REVISE EDEXCEL GCSE
Religious Studies
Religion & Life (Unit 1) and Religion & Society (Unit 8) Christianity & Islam

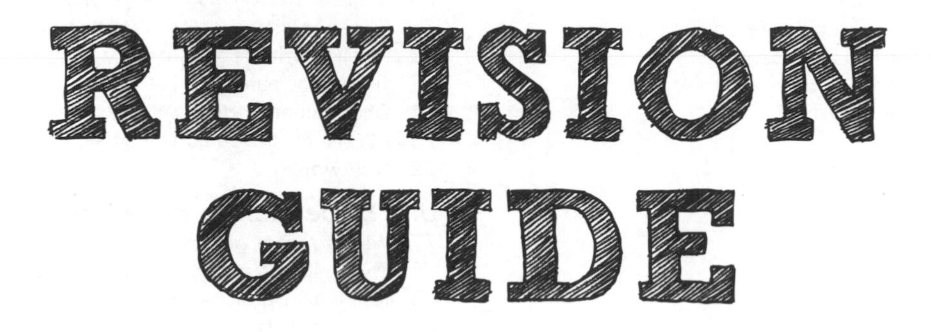

Series Consultant: Harry Smith

Author: Tanya Hill

A note from the publisher

In order to ensure that this resource offers high-quality support for the associated Edexcel qualification, it has been through a review process by the awarding body to confirm that it fully covers the teaching and learning content of the specification or part of a specification at which it is aimed, and demonstrates an appropriate balance between the development of subject skills, knowledge and understanding, in addition to preparation for assessment.

While the publishers have made every attempt to ensure that advice on the qualification and its assessment is accurate, the official specification and associated assessment guidance materials are the only authoritative source of information and should always be referred to for definitive guidance.

Edexcel examiners have not contributed to any sections in this resource relevant to examination papers for which they have responsibility.

No material from an endorsed resource will be used verbatim in any assessment set by Edexcel.

Endorsement of a resource does not mean that the resource is required to achieve this Edexcel qualification, nor does it mean that it is the only suitable material available to support the qualification, and any resource lists produced by the awarding body shall include this and other appropriate resources.

Contents

1-to-1 page match with the Revision Workbook ISBN 9781446905289

A small bit of small print

Edexcel publishes Sample Assessment Material and the Specification on its website. This is the official content and this book should be used in conjunction with it. The questions in *Now try this* have been written to help you practise every topic in the book. Remember: the real exam questions may not look like this.

Key words

All the key words on the GCSE Religious Studies Specification are highlighted in red in this book. Definitions can be found on pages 11, 24, 36, 48, 64, 76, 88 and 100.

Introduction

People hold different views about God and it is important to understand the reasons why this is.

AGNOSTICISM

This means not being sure whether God exists. A person who holds this view is called an **agnostic**.

ATHEISM

The belief that God does not exist. A person who holds this view is called an **atheist**.

What do Christians believe?

Christians believe God:

- is omnipotent (all-powerful), omniscient (all-knowing) and omni-benevolent (all-good)
- created the world and everything in it.
- answers prayers and can perform miracles.

You'll come across more examples of Christian and non-Christian beliefs as you go through this book.

Why do atheists not believe in God?

Atheists may offer many reasons but some common reasons are:

- **Science**, not religion, explains how the world was created.
- There is no physical proof of God's existence.
- Many events that theists believe are due to God (such as **miracles**) can be explained by science or as coincidences.
- Evil and suffering in the world prove that an all-loving and all-powerful God cannot exist.

Why are some people agnostic?

Agnostics are unsure about God's existence because they believe there is no reliable evidence either in support of God's existence or against it.

EXAM ALERT!

Many students get confused between the words '**atheism**' and '**agnosticism**'. Create yourself some key words cards with the key term on one side and the definitions and reasons for this view on the other to help you revise them.

Students have struggled with this topic in recent exams – **be prepared!** ResultsPlus

Now try this

1 What is **atheism**? (a, 2 marks)
2 What does **omnipotence** mean? (a, 2 marks)

There are extra marks available for Section 1 of Unit 1, so make sure you leave time to check your spelling, punctuation and grammar, and to check that you have used key words where possible.

Religious upbringing

Many people believe in God because of the way in which they have been brought up.

The reasons why Christian families raise their children to believe in God

- Christians believe it is their duty to marry, have a family and raise their children within the Christian faith.
- Christians believe their religion gives children a secure basis and helps them through difficulties.

Sometimes as children grow up and are introduced to different ideas and beliefs, they may feel the religion with which they were raised is not the correct choice for them. This can be difficult for parents to accept.

How do Christian families encourage their children to believe in God?

Baptism

A child is **welcomed** into the Church with family, friends and the worshipping congregation promising to support them within the Christian faith.

Worship

Children attend Sunday School to **learn** about Jesus, God and the Church. They also attend Church services and celebrate Christian festivals.

Confirmation

A child will be encouraged to **confirm** and renew the vows made for them in Baptism when they are old enough to make this decision for themselves.

School

Christian parents may choose a Church school that helps to **educate** children in the Christian faith.

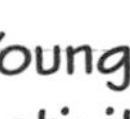

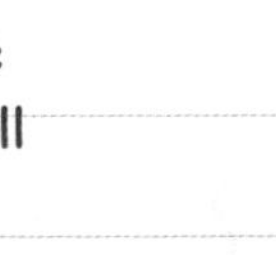

Parents' examples

Through their own **examples**, Christian parents will encourage their children to believe in God. By seeing their parents praying, hearing about God through Bible stories and attending Church, children will be more likely to believe in God.

Community

Young Christians can meet and share in activities such as Bible study groups, youth clubs, prayer meetings or other events. This offers a sense of **belonging** and community. Young adults are supported by the Church and may also meet partners in the Church community.

Now try this

1 Explain how a religious upbringing can lead to belief in God. **(c, 8 marks)**

2 'Parents should not force their religion onto their children.' In your answer you should refer to at least one religion.

(i) Do you agree? Give reasons for your opinion. **(d, 3 marks)**

(ii) Give reasons why some people may disagree with you. **(3 marks)**

All 'explain' questions require you to go into depth in your answer. For success in this question, show you understand what it means to have a religious upbringing, and also show why this may lead to a belief in God.

In the exam, you are given plenty of space to answer these (d) style questions so use it! Try to give **three** reasons for your opinion and make sure you refer to a specific religion.

Religious experiences

Some people believe in God because they have had a religious experience. This **convinces** them that God exists. This page will help you revise the four main types of religious experience and how these may lead to belief in God.

Numinous experience

An experience which completely amazes someone and often inspires **awe** and **wonder**. Usually words are not enough to describe the experience but it leaves a person aware of a being greater than themselves.

Conversion

An experience that causes an individual to **change** their beliefs, ideas or complete lifestyle. An atheist may suddenly become a believer in God or a person may change from one religion to another.

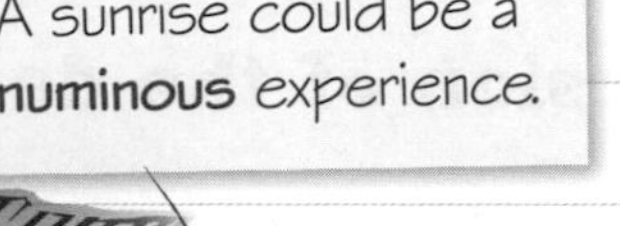

A sunrise could be a **numinous** experience.

Types of religious experience

In the Bible Saul originally persecuted Christians. After his **conversion** experience he became a Christian.

3 Prayer

A method which believers use to **communicate** with God. Prayer can be personal, or can be a group experience when believers worship together. Believers pray to share their ideas with God, to praise him, to thank him for what he has provided, to ask for forgiveness or to show gratitude.

4 Miracles

An **act of God** that appears to be impossible as it goes against the laws of nature. It is usually performed for a religious reason.

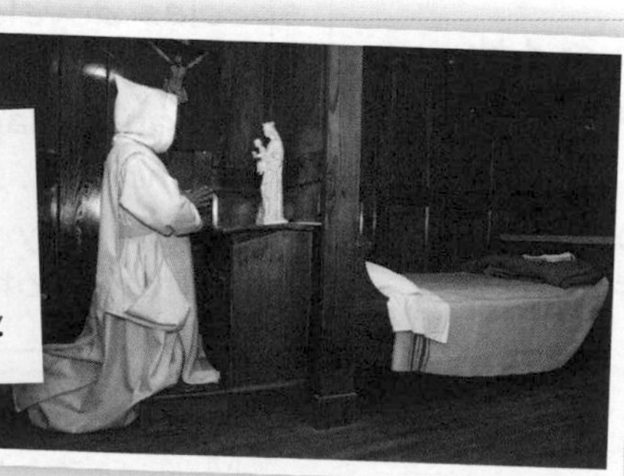

Carmelite monks have an hour of silent morning prayer every day.

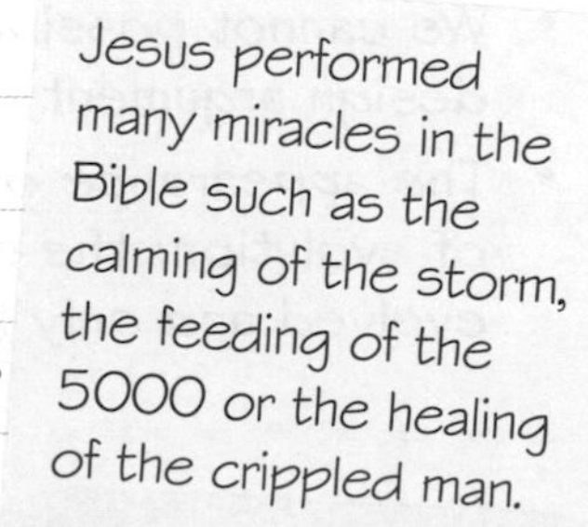

Jesus performed many miracles in the Bible such as the calming of the storm, the feeding of the 5000 or the healing of the crippled man.

Now try this

1 What is meant by a **numinous experience**? **(a, 2 marks)**

2 Do you think God answers prayers?
Give two reasons for your point of view. **(b, 4 marks)**

This question asks for your **opinion** on the given topic. You must give two different and well thought out reasons for your view. Try to explain each one carefully.

Had a look ☐ Nearly there ☐ Nailed it! ☐

The design argument

The design argument tries to prove the existence of God by arguing that the universe was designed. This leads some people to believe in God.

Overview of the design argument

Design is the result of intelligent thought → The universe shows evidence of being designed (e.g. gravity, ozone layer) → This suggests that a being with intelligence designed the universe → The universe is too complex to have happened by chance or be designed by any being other than God → Therefore God exists

Paley's Watch: William Paley's version of the design argument

1 Paley compared the world to a watch.

2 If a person saw a watch for the first time he or she would immediately know it had been designed because it is so complex.

3 A watch has many parts that have been carefully made and put together to work successfully, so it must have been planned and designed.

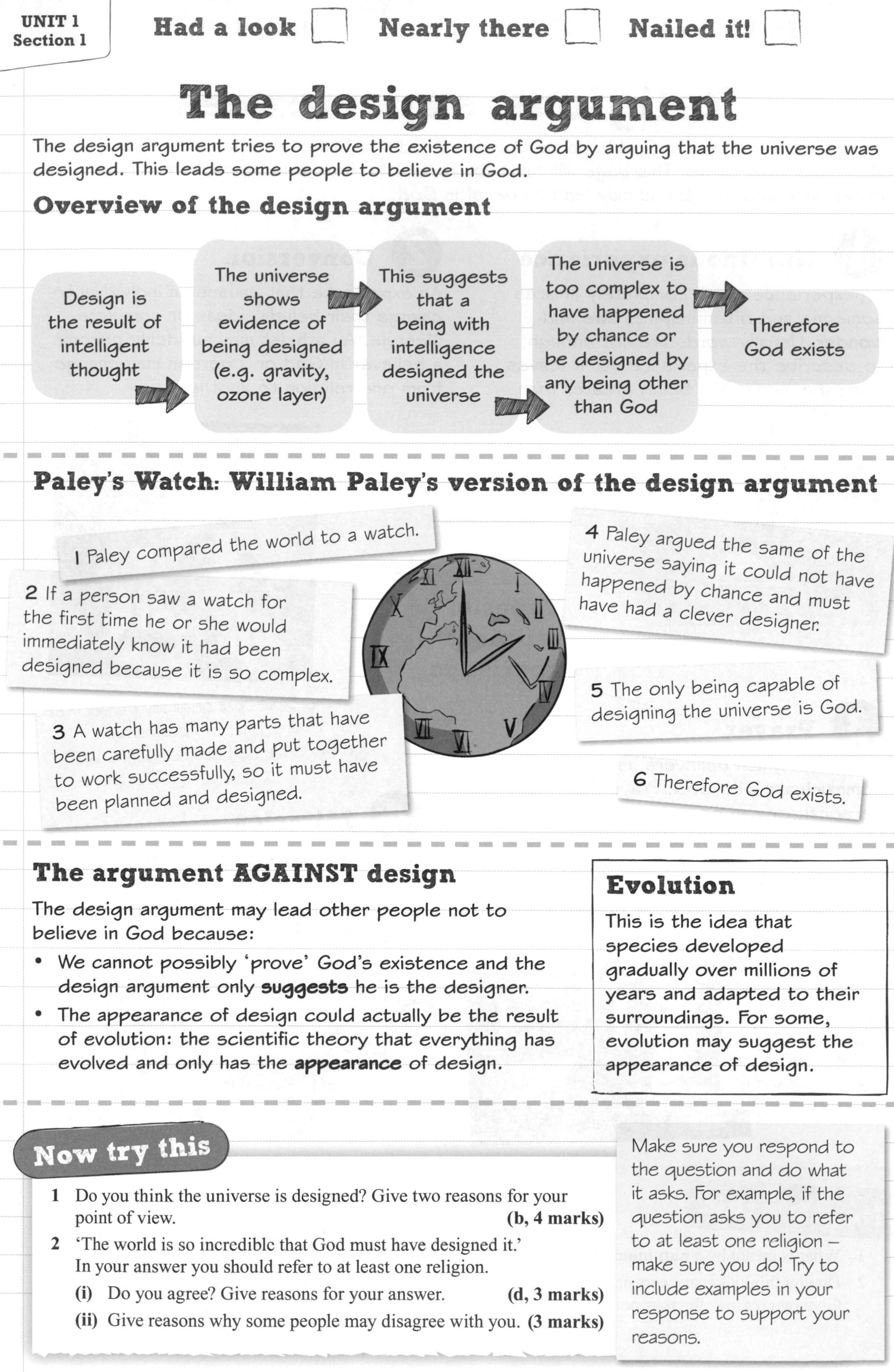

4 Paley argued the same of the universe saying it could not have happened by chance and must have had a clever designer.

5 The only being capable of designing the universe is God.

6 Therefore God exists.

The argument AGAINST design

The design argument may lead other people not to believe in God because:

- We cannot possibly 'prove' God's existence and the design argument only **suggests** he is the designer.
- The appearance of design could actually be the result of evolution: the scientific theory that everything has evolved and only has the **appearance** of design.

Evolution

This is the idea that species developed gradually over millions of years and adapted to their surroundings. For some, evolution may suggest the appearance of design.

Now try this

1 Do you think the universe is designed? Give two reasons for your point of view. **(b, 4 marks)**

2 'The world is so incredible that God must have designed it.'
In your answer you should refer to at least one religion.
(i) Do you agree? Give reasons for your answer. **(d, 3 marks)**
(ii) Give reasons why some people may disagree with you. **(3 marks)**

Make sure you respond to the question and do what it asks. For example, if the question asks you to refer to at least one religion – make sure you do! Try to include examples in your response to support your reasons.

The causation argument

The causation argument tries to prove the existence of God by showing that everything happens for a reason. This leads some people to believe in God.

Overview of the causation argument

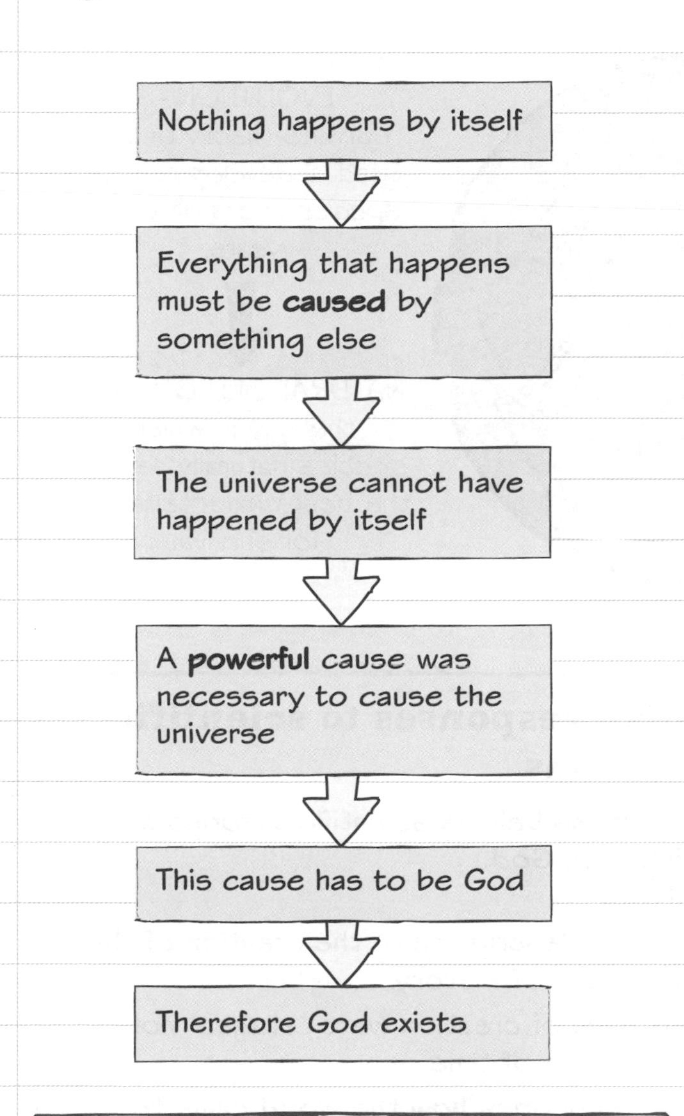

The Big Bang theory

This is the idea that an enormous explosion started the universe around 15 billion years ago.

The cosmological argument

This is another name for the causation argument. In the 13th century, Thomas Aquinas argued that everything that happens is caused by something else. However, he argued that you cannot go back indefinitely and that there must have been a first cause of the universe. Aquinas believed this first cause had to be God and called him the '**unmoved mover**' because he is the start of the universe.

Arguments AGAINST causation

- The causation argument cannot be proved.
- Even if everything in the world seems to have a cause, it doesn't mean the universe had a cause.
- The argument only suggests that God is the cause of the universe.
- There are other possible causes of the universe such as the scientific 'Big Bang' theory.
- If everything has a cause, what caused God?

Now try this

1 Do you think God is the cause of the universe? Give two reasons for your point of view. **(b, 4 marks)**

2 Explain how the causation argument may lead to belief in God. **(c, 8 marks)**

To answer these questions think about why many religious believers think God caused the universe and the evidence that suggests this claim is true.

To give the best answers to all (c) questions on your Unit 1 paper, make sure you check that your answers make sense and that what you want to say is very clear.

Had a look ☐ Nearly there ☐ Nailed it! ☐

Scientific explanations of the origins of the world

The main scientific explanation for the origins of the world is The Big Bang Theory. Evolution and Natural Selection explain the origin of the species. These lead some people to believe that there is no God.

Scientific explanations

'BIG BANG' THEORY – an enormous explosion started the universe around 15 billion years ago.

EVOLUTION – Darwin's theory of the gradual development of species over millions of years.

NATURAL SELECTION – the way in which species naturally select the best characteristics for survival.

Is there a God?

Scientific theories about the origins of the universe lead some people to **doubt** God's existence because:

- They offer **alternative** explanations of how the world and humans came to exist, with no reference to God.
- Science offers **evidence** that can be seen and tested whereas God cannot be seen or proven in the same way.

Christian responses to scientific explanations

Some Christians believe scientific theories are **compatible** with God.
They believe:

- The Bible's description of the creation of the world is more of a story.
- The six days of creation were 'stages' not actual periods of time.
- Science describes **how** the world came to exist and the Bible explains **why**.

Other Christians believe that scientific explanations of the world are **wrong** because they conflict with what is written in the Bible. These Christians are called creationists.

Now try this

1 'Scientific explanations of the existence of the world prove God did not create it'. In your answer you should refer to at least one religion.

(i) Do you agree? Give reasons for your opinion. **(d, 3 marks)**

(ii) Give reasons why some people may disagree with you. **(3 marks)**

Spend time reading the statement to make sure you properly understand it before you answer the questions.

Unanswered prayers

Unanswered prayers may lead some people to question whether there is a God.

The problem with unanswered prayers

1. Prayers are **communication** with God. If they are not answered, people might think God is not listening.

2. Many people who experience pain and suffering in their lives pray to God, but if God does nothing about it, they may feel their prayers have been unanswered.

3. Unanswered prayers may lead some Christians to **question** their belief in God, to reject him or believe he does not exist.

EXAM ALERT!

When writing responses to questions on unanswered prayers, try to think about why this might pose a challenge to faith, why this may convince some atheists that God does not exist as well as considering reasons why God does not answer all prayers.

Also, remember that if you are answering a (b) or (d) part (i) question, you need to give your own opinion first.

Students have struggled with this topic in recent exams – **be prepared!** ResultsPlus

Christian responses to unanswered prayers

Now try this

1 What is **prayer**? **(a, 2 marks)**

2 Explain how Christians may respond to the problem of unanswered prayers. **(c, 8 marks)**

To be successful on (a) questions, make sure you learn the key words thoroughly.

The best answers offer a **full** explanation of how different Christians respond when their prayers are not answered. You could also try to give examples to support your answers.

Had a look ☐ Nearly there ☐ Nailed it! ☐

The problem of evil and suffering

Evil and suffering cause a problem for people who believe in God. Some of them may stop believing in God.

What is evil and suffering?

There are two main types of evil and suffering:

Not all suffering is caused by evil because sometimes a person's choices and actions can cause suffering (for example drug abuse).

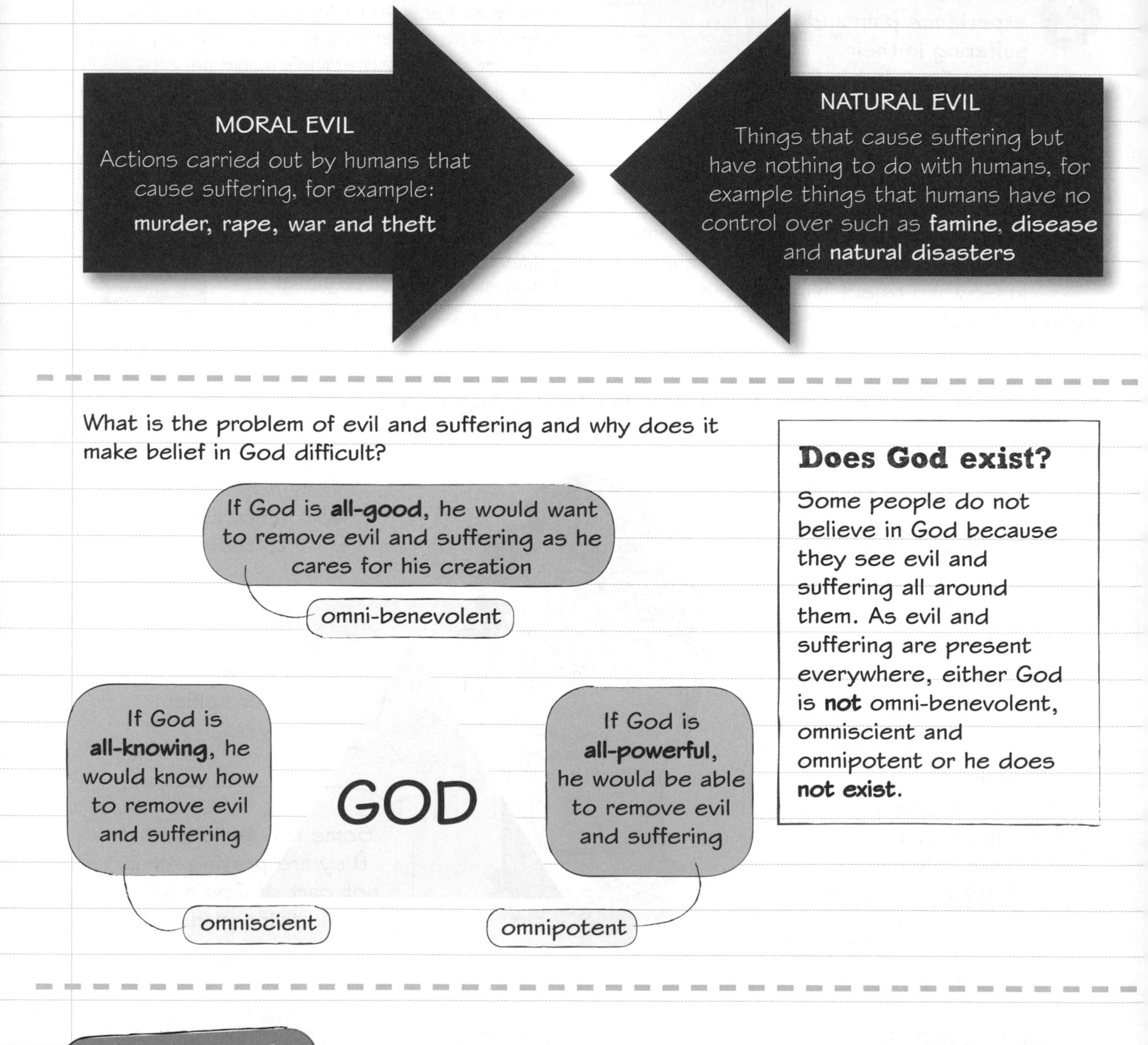

What is the problem of evil and suffering and why does it make belief in God difficult?

If God is **all-good**, he would want to remove evil and suffering as he cares for his creation — omni-benevolent

If God is **all-knowing**, he would know how to remove evil and suffering — omniscient

GOD

If God is **all-powerful**, he would be able to remove evil and suffering — omnipotent

Does God exist?

Some people do not believe in God because they see evil and suffering all around them. As evil and suffering are present everywhere, either God is **not** omni-benevolent, omniscient and omnipotent or he does **not exist.**

Now try this

1 What is **moral evil**? **(a, 2 marks)**

2 Explain why evil and suffering suggest that God does not exist. **(c, 8 marks)**

Use the triangle diagram above to help you answer this question successfully.

Christian responses to the problem of evil and suffering

Christians respond to the problem of evil and suffering in different ways and look to the Bible for guidance.

What does the Bible say about evil and suffering?

Free will – the idea that humans are free to make their own choices.

- Genesis says that God created a perfect world.
- The fall: Adam and Eve used their free will in the Garden of Eden to disobey God which allowed evil and suffering to enter the world.
- Christians believe God sent Jesus to Earth to overcome the evil in the world and die for the sins of humanity on the cross.

Christian explanations

Christians offer **explanations** for evil and suffering that allow them to still believe in God.

1. **Free will:** God gave people free will. This is the ability to make choices for themselves. Some accept that evil and suffering can be the result of free will.
2. **Test from God:** Some Christians accept that evil and suffering may be a test from God. Believers are allowed to go through difficult times to see how they react. Some become stronger, for example.

3. **God's plan:** suffering happens for a reason: Evil and suffering are part of God's plan. People should trust God because he knows why everything happens.

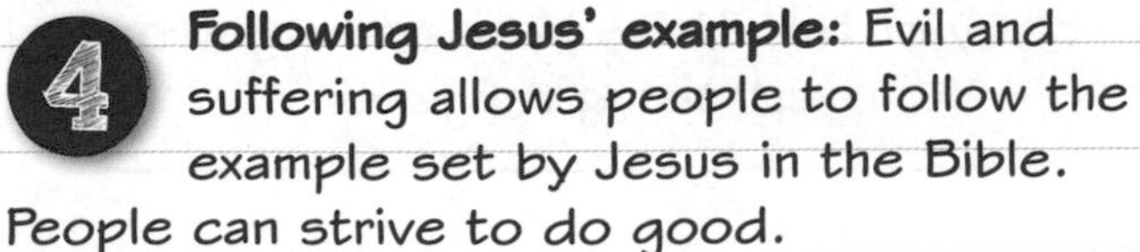

4. **Following Jesus' example:** Evil and suffering allows people to follow the example set by Jesus in the Bible. People can strive to do good.

Christian responses

Christians may respond by:

Christian responses

- **Praying** – hoping God will give them the strength to cope with what they face or praying for others.
- **Helping others** – for example becoming a doctor or nurse so they can help others cope with suffering.
- **Volunteering** – with a charity or organisation that supports others when they are suffering.
- **Strengthening their faith** – with the knowledge God has a plan for them.

Now try this

1 Do you think the presence of evil and suffering in the world proves God does not exist? Give two reasons for your point of view. **(b, 4 marks)**

2 'It is possible to accept evil and suffering and still believe in God'.

(i) Do you agree? Give reasons for your opinion. **(d, 3 marks)**

(ii) Give reasons why some people may disagree with you. **(3 marks)**

Had a look ☐ Nearly there ☐ Nailed it! ☐

The media and belief in God

There are many different ways in which the media portray belief in God. These can affect attitudes towards believing in God.

Examples of media programmes or films about religion

	Songs of Praise – shows worship in a church, speaks to famous stars who are religious, and teaches about religion and religious ideas *The Vicar of Dibley* – a sitcom which features a female vicar and deals with many religious ideas Documentaries, for example *Tsunami – Where was God?*: a documentary questioning the existence of God in the face of evil and suffering
	Many radio stations feature a segment about worship or religion, whether it is a 'Thought for the Day' or highlighting of a religious idea
	Bruce Almighty – based around the idea of taking on the job of God *The Da Vinci Code* – dealing with issues to do with Jesus and hidden religious ideas

You need to know **two** examples of the media that deal with religious issues and identify what impact they may have on the viewer and their beliefs about God.

The media's effect on attitudes to and belief in God

The media can have a powerful influence on how we view the world, including Christianity.

POSITIVE
Some religious programmes show how religion can **benefit** the life of an individual and how it can be a **positive** thing.

NEGATIVE
Some religious programmes can portray religion as something to laugh at and **ridicule**, or question God's existence. They may suggest religious believers are crazy or that there is something **wrong** with being religious.

Now try this

1 Do you think television programmes encourage people to believe in God? Give two reasons for your point of view. **(b, 4 marks)**

2 'The media shows a positive image of religion today.'

(i) Do you agree? Give reasons for your opinion. **(d, 3 marks)**

(ii) Give reasons why some people may disagree with you. **(3 marks)**

Make sure you consider how the media may affect someone's faith, rather than just describing the programme.

Key words

It is important that you learn the key words for each topic. This is so you can explain what they mean for (a) type questions and use the key words in your answers to other questions to explain ideas fully.

Key words	Definitions
agnosticism	not being sure whether God exists
atheism	believing that God does not exist
conversion	when your life is changed by giving yourself to God
free will	the idea that humans are free to make their own choices
miracle	something which seems to break a law of science and makes you think only God could have done it
moral evil	actions done by humans which causes suffering
natural evil	things which cause suffering but have nothing to do with humans
numinous	the feeling of the presence of something greater than you
omni-benevolent	the belief that God is all-good
omnipotent	the belief that God is all-powerful
omniscient	the belief that God knows everything that has happened and everything that is going to happen
prayer	an attempt to contact God, usually through words

Had a look ☐ Nearly there ☐ Nailed it! ☐

Christian beliefs in life after death

All Christians believe there is an afterlife for those who believe in God.

Why Christians believe in life after death

Most Christians believe that after death the body stays in the grave and the soul goes to God for **judgement**. Those that have been good will go to **Heaven**, and the souls of unrepentant sinners will go to **Hell**. Catholics also believe in **purgatory** and that the body will be **resurrected**. The idea that souls live on after death is called immortality of the soul.

Protestants	Evangelical Christians	Roman Catholics
Evidence	Evidence	Evidence
• Jesus told a thief on the cross that he would be in heaven that day. • Jesus said his father's house had many rooms. • The Church teaches that all Christians, dead and alive, belong to the Church. • Some Christians think the paranormal (e.g. ghosts and mediums) is evidence of an afterlife.	• Jesus' body was raised from the dead. • The creed (St Paul): 'I believe in the resurrection of the body and everlasting life'.	• Resurrection of Jesus. • Teaching of the New Testament e.g. the Book of Revelation. • Teaching of the Catechism of the Catholic Church. • The creed which says Jesus 'is seated at the right hand of the father and will come again to judge the living and the dead'.

Differences in belief

Protestants: some Protestants believe that there is no Hell.

Roman Catholics: believe in Purgatory, where the souls of sinners are sent to be cleansed. The souls of those who do not believe in God or who have committed unforgiveable sins will go to Hell. When the world ends, Jesus returns to earth to raise the dead (resurrection), God will make a new Heaven and the souls still in purgatory will go to Heaven.

Now try this

1 What is meant by **immortality of the soul**? **(a, 2 marks)**

2 Do you think there is a life after death? Give two reasons for your point of view. **(b, 4 marks)**

The effect of belief in the afterlife on Christians lives

Belief in life after death affects the way Christians live their lives. They believe that God will reward those who have lived according to his will.

The effect on Christian lives

Christians try to live within the **guidelines** of the Bible and the Church.
This affects how they live and how they treat people.

How might Christians respond in their lives?

1. **Confession** – repent for their sins
2. **Prayer** – praying more regularly and communicate more frequently with God
3. **Doing good work** – because they know God is watching them, they will try to live life how he wants them to by helping others
4. **Putting Christian teachings into action** – they will follow God's commandments and the example of Jesus through 'treating others as they would like to be treated'
5. **Vocation** – they may choose to dedicate their lives to God through jobs such as a nurse or doctor and helping others or by becoming a priest or minister, nun or monk

Now try this

1 Explain how beliefs about life after death may affect the actions of a Christian. **(c, 8 marks)**

Try to write a **new paragraph** for each point you make. This makes it easier to go back and check that you have said what you wanted to say and that your answer makes sense.

Had a look ☐ Nearly there ☐ Nailed it! ☐

Islamic beliefs about life after death

Muslims believe in *akhirah* (life after death). It is one of the main beliefs of Islam that makes a person a Muslim. This has an effect on the life of a Muslim.

Muslim beliefs about *akhirah*

After death, the angel of death will take a person's soul to *barzakh* (the stage between when a person dies and when they face judgement).

→ Allah will judge each individual on the way they lived their life.

→ On the Day of Judgement the body will be resurrected.

→ Two angels will open the book which contains the record of what a person has done in their lifetime.

→ If their name is recorded on the right-hand side of the book, they will be sent to *al'Jannah* (paradise).

→ If their name is recorded on the left-hand side of the book, they will be sent to *Jahannam* (Hell).

Why Muslims believe in the afterlife:

- The authority of the Qur'an. The Qur'an states that we came from Allah and we must return to Allah.
- Surahs 11 and 56 teach that those who live a good life will go to *al'Jannah* and that Allah is powerful but also merciful.
- The teaching and practice of the Prophet (the *Sunnah*).

Judgement:

- The Qur'an and Shari'ah law teach that Muslims will be judged by Allah and their actions will determine their afterlife.
- Islam teaches that the good will be rewarded and the evil punished.
- The Qur'an teaches that God's judgement is final.
- Only the judgement of Allah puts the wrongs of life right.

The effect on the life of a Muslim:

- All Muslims try to follow the teachings of the **Qur'an and Shari'ah law**.
- They will also follow the **example** of Prophet Muhammad and try to be a good Muslim.
- They will try to act the way Allah wishes, caring for others and not causing harm.
- Muslims believe Allah sees everything they do and they will be **judged** on this in the afterlife so will try to please him.

Now try this

1 Choose one religion other than Christianity and explain why the followers believe in life after death. **(c, 8 marks)**

2 Choose one religion other than Christianity and explain how a belief in life after death affects the way its followers choose to lead their lives. **(c, 8 marks)**

Make sure you read the question carefully. These two (c) questions look the same but ask for different things. The first question asks you to explain **why** followers believe in life after death. The second question asks you to explain the **effect** of these beliefs on followers' lives.

Non-religious beliefs in life after death

Some people who are not religious still believe in an afterlife. You need to know what the reasons are and be able to give your opinion on this.

Non-religious reasons for belief in an afterlife

NEAR-DEATH EXPERIENCES

- Near-death experiences are reported by patients pronounced dead for a short time.
- They describe leaving their bodies and seeing themselves outside of their body.
- Sometimes people have reported seeing dead relatives or a bright light.

PARANORMAL ACTIVITY

- Paranormal activity refers to unexplained events that are thought to have a spiritual cause.
- Ghosts are thought to be spirits of dead people who have not travelled to 'the next place'. Evidence can be a physical presence that cannot be seen or a feeling of something being in the room with you.
- Mediums claim to be able to contact the dead. You can attend meetings (séances) where people believe this happens. Some people claim these are not real.

REINCARNATION

- Reincarnation is the belief that a person's soul is reborn into another body or form after death.
- An idea believed by Sikhs and Hindus but also by many non-religious people because of memories from the past or déjà vu.

Other reasons why people believe in an afterlife

- The idea of death is **difficult** to deal with.
- Belief in an afterlife seems to make life **fairer**.
- Sometimes people feel their loved ones who have died are still with them.
- It makes sense that those who have led a good life should be rewarded and those who have not should be punished.

Now try this

1 'The paranormal proves that there must be life after death'.
In your answer you should refer to at least one religion.

(i) Do you agree? Give reasons for your answer. **(d, 3 marks)**

(ii) Give reasons why some people may disagree with you. **(3 marks)**

Use the content above to help you answer this question. Remember to give relevant reasons with examples for both parts of the question.

Non-belief in life after death

Some people reject all ideas of an afterlife and you need to understand why this is.

Evidence

- There is no evidence of an afterlife – no one has ever returned to prove it exists.
- Mediums and others who try to prove there is an afterlife are tricking people.

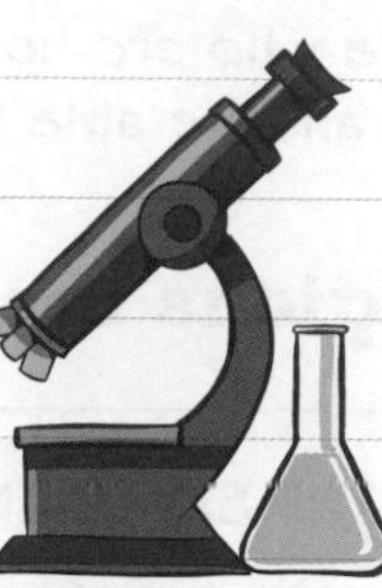

Different reasons for not believing in life after death

Science

- Science explains everything in our world and we should not believe in things that are unscientific.

Humans are mortal

- When a person dies their body decays so how can there be anything else?
- Life after death is impossible – we live and then die.

Religion is outdated

- Beliefs in Heaven and Hell are outdated and were ideas used to control people and their behaviour in the past.
- Religion offers no good evidence of an afterlife.
- The Bible, which contains this information, is not as relevant today.
- Some argue God is not real and it does not make sense to believe in life after death without reference to God.

EXAM ALERT!

Students answering questions on why some people do not believe in any sort of an afterlife often give vague and not very well thought out reasons. The best answers will include different reasons why **no** belief in the afterlife is held and the reasons will be developed.

Students have struggled with this topic in recent exams – **be prepared!** ResultsPlus

Now try this

1 Explain why many non-religious people do not believe in any kind of afterlife. **(c, 8 marks)**

To be successful on this question, take time to answer the question thoroughly. Use the information on this page to help you, making sure you use the correct vocabulary and evidence/examples to support your answer.

Abortion

An abortion is the removal of a foetus from the womb before it can survive. It is when a pregnancy is ended by surgical or medical means.

When does life begin?

The issue of abortion is controversial because there are many views about when life might begin.

- At fertilisation – when the egg and sperm meet?
- When the fertised egg is implanted into the womb?
- When the foetus is developing in the womb?
- When the foetus is capable of living independantly of the mother?
- At birth?
- At some other point?

The UK abortion laws

1967 Abortion Act
Human Fertilisation and Embryology Act of 1990

- Abortions must be agreed by two doctors.

Abortion is allowed ***up to*** 24 weeks if:

- there is a physical or mental risk to the woman's health.
- any existing children would suffer or be at risk.
- the child born would be severely disabled.

Abortion is allowed ***after*** 24 weeks if:

- there is risk to the mother's life.
- the baby will be severely deformed.
- there would be risk of serious physical or mental injury to the woman.

Arguments FOR abortion (Pro-choice)

✔ Women should have the **right** to choose – it is their body.
✔ In cases of rape, abortion should be allowed.
✔ It is **kinder** to allow abortion if the child will be severely disabled.
✔ Babies have the right to be loved and cared for and the woman cannot always provide this.

Arguments AGAINST abortion (Pro-life)

✗ Life begins at **conception**.
✗ An embryo has the potential to be a human and should have the **right to life**.
✗ Even disabled children have the right to life.
✗ Adoption is an alternative.

Now try this

1 What is **abortion**? **(a, 2 marks)**
2 Do you think abortion should be legal in the UK today? Give two reasons for your point of view. **(b, 4 marks)**

Remember, abortion is a complex issue because it is not clear when life actually begins so make sure you reflect this idea in any answers you write about abortion.

Had a look ☐ Nearly there ☐ Nailed it! ☐

Christian attitudes to abortion

Christians may hold different views about abortion, although most will not support abortion because of the 'sanctity of life'.

'Sanctity of life' argument

This is the belief that life is sacred and belongs to God.

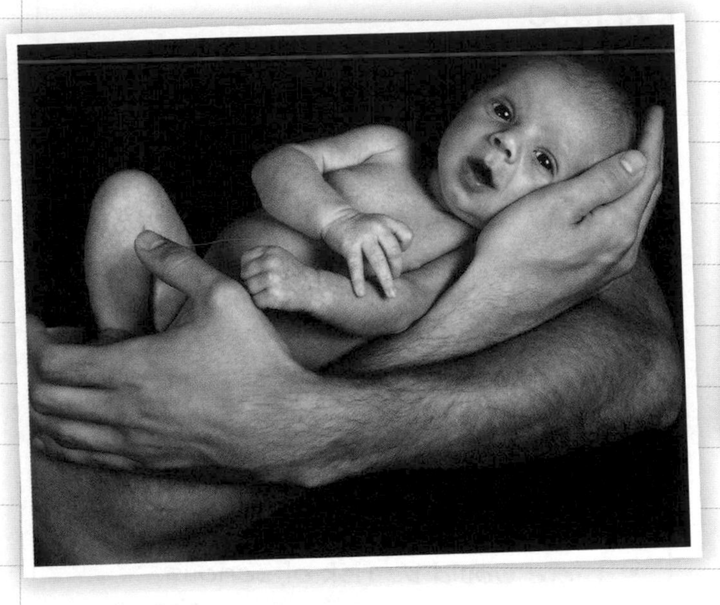

There are important passages in the Bible that support the sanctity of life argument:

'So God created man in his own image'.
Genesis 1:27

'Your body is a temple of the Holy Spirit...'
1 Corinthians 6:19

'You shall not commit murder'.
Exodus 20:13

Arguments AGAINST abortion

Some Christians (such as Catholics and Evangelical Protestants) do not support abortion because:

- ✗ Abortion is viewed as **murder**.
- ✗ Life is a **sacred** gift from God.
- ✗ God has a **plan** for every human.
- ✗ All life has **value** even if a child may be born disabled.
- ✗ Life begins at conception.

Arguments FOR abortion

Some other Christians are more liberal, agreeing abortion is not good but that sometimes it is the 'lesser of two evils'.

They argue:

- ✔ Jesus taught about **compassion** towards others.
- ✔ We cannot be sure life begins at conception.
- ✔ In cases of rape or incest, it is the kindest action.
- ✔ Medical technology allows us to identify problems with the foetus.
- ✔ Abortion is the best choice if the mother's life is at risk.

Now try this

1. What is meant by **sanctity of life**? **(a, 2 marks)**
2. Explain why some Christians agree with abortion and some do not. **(c, 8 marks)**

Some 'Explain' questions ask you to give one point of view, whereas others ask you to give two points, as here. This question also refers to Christians in particular. Make sure you read the question carefully so that you can give the right answer.

Muslim attitudes to abortion

Muslims share similar ideas to Christians about the sanctity of life and abortion. However, there are circumstances in which abortion is allowed.

SANCTITY OF LIFE
Life for Muslims is **sacred** and a gift from God. Abortion takes away a life so is wrong

ENSOULMENT
Life begins when the **soul** has entered the foetus at 120 days. Some Muslims claim this happens earlier, after 40 days

'Whoever has spared the life of a soul, it is as though he has spared the life of all people. Whosoever has killed a soul, it is as though he has murdered all of mankind'.
Qur'an 5:32

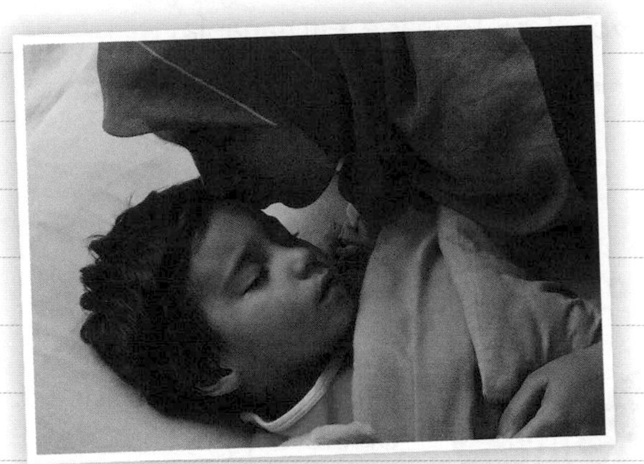

When is abortion allowed?

Muslims believe abortion is wrong but many believe it might be allowed in some cases (for example if the mother's life is in danger). This is because:

- the foetus would not exist if it was not for the mother
- the mother's life is established and she has responsibilities to carry out.

Different Muslim views on abortion

- Some Muslims allow abortion in the first 16 weeks, others only in the first 7 weeks of pregnancy.
- Before ensoulment (120 days) a foetus known to be suffering from a serious defect or blood disorder can be aborted.
- Some argue abortion is allowed in cases of rape or incest.
- Some Muslim women believe they should be able to **choose** what happens to their bodies.
- Abortion is never allowed in situations where parents are concerned that they cannot care for the child.
- An unplanned pregnancy is not a reason for abortion.
- Abortion is also not allowed if the pregnancy is a result of **adultery**.
- After 120 days, abortion is only permitted if the mother's life is in **danger**.

Now try this

1 'Religious believers should never accept abortion.'
In your answer you should refer to at least one religion.
(i) Do you agree? Give reasons for your opinion. **(d, 3 marks)**
(ii) Give reasons why some people may disagree with you. **(3 marks)**

Make sure you separate the two parts of your answer (and the two different opinions) and that they are clearly different.

Euthanasia

Euthanasia is the painless killing of someone dying from a painful disease. This is a controversial issue because some view it as murder whereas others see it as helping someone to carry out their wishes.

Types of euthanasia

- Voluntary euthanasia = a person's life is ended deliberately and painlessly at their request.
- Assisted suicide = providing a seriously ill person with the means to commit suicide.
- Non-voluntary euthanasia = ending someone's life painlessly when they are unable to ask, but you have good reason for thinking they would want you to do so.

Euthanasia in the UK

- All forms of euthanasia are **against** the law.
- Switching off a life support machine for a patient who is 'brain dead' is not considered euthanasia and **is** allowed.
- In 1993, the House of Lords rejected a proposal to legalise euthanasia.

Ways in which euthanasia is carried out

Active euthanasia – carried out by a doctor performing a deliberate action such as a lethal injection.

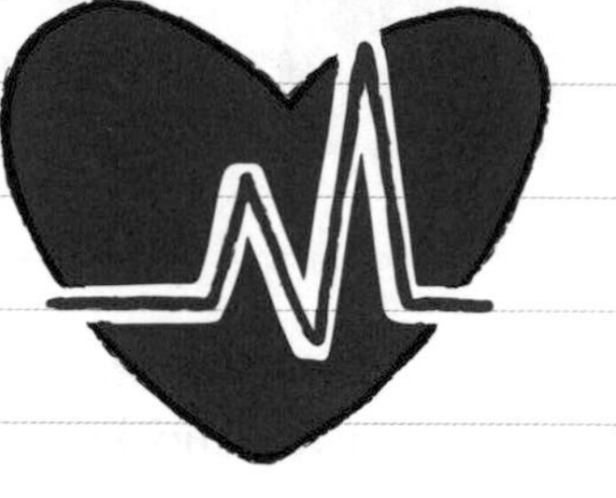

Passive euthanasia – when medical treatment or life support is withdrawn or when a severely ill person is not given treatment to help them survive.

Arguments FOR euthanasia

✔ Allows the patient to die a gentle, pain-free death.

✔ The patient dies with **dignity**.

✔ Euthanasia saves medical costs.

✔ Medical staff can focus on patients with more chance of recovery.

✔ It relieves the family burden.

Arguments AGAINST euthanasia

✘ Sanctity of life – life is **sacred** and special.

✘ Slippery slope – if euthanasia were legalised, it would lead to other things being made legal which would lessen the value of life.

✘ Some people may be pressurised into choosing euthanasia.

✘ Hospices provide alternative palliative care for patients so euthanasia is not needed.

✘ Doctors can be wrong about a diagnosis.

✘ Helping someone to commit suicide means living with what you have done for the rest of your life.

Now try this

1 What is **assisted suicide**? **(a, 2 marks)**

2 Do you think euthanasia should be legal in the UK? Give two reasons for your answer. **(b, 4 marks)**

Christian attitudes to euthanasia

In the way that many Christians do not accept abortion, they also do not accept euthanasia.

Is it ever right?

Some Christians are more accepting of euthanasia. They support the view that God intends people to have a good quality of life, which people considering euthanasia often do not have. Some might argue that euthanasia in this case is the lesser of two evils.

Hospice movement

Hospices provide good quality pain relief, support the dying and their families, and help the dying prepare for death.

Hospices are seen by some Christians as an alternative to euthanasia.

HOSPICE
Peace, Comfort and Dignity

Now try this

1 Explain why some Christians agree with euthanasia and some do not. **(c, 8 marks)**

Try to show you understand both sides of the debate in your answer and show why it is not straightforward.

Had a look ☐ Nearly there ☐ Nailed it! ☐

Muslim attitudes to euthanasia

For Muslims euthanasia is always wrong.

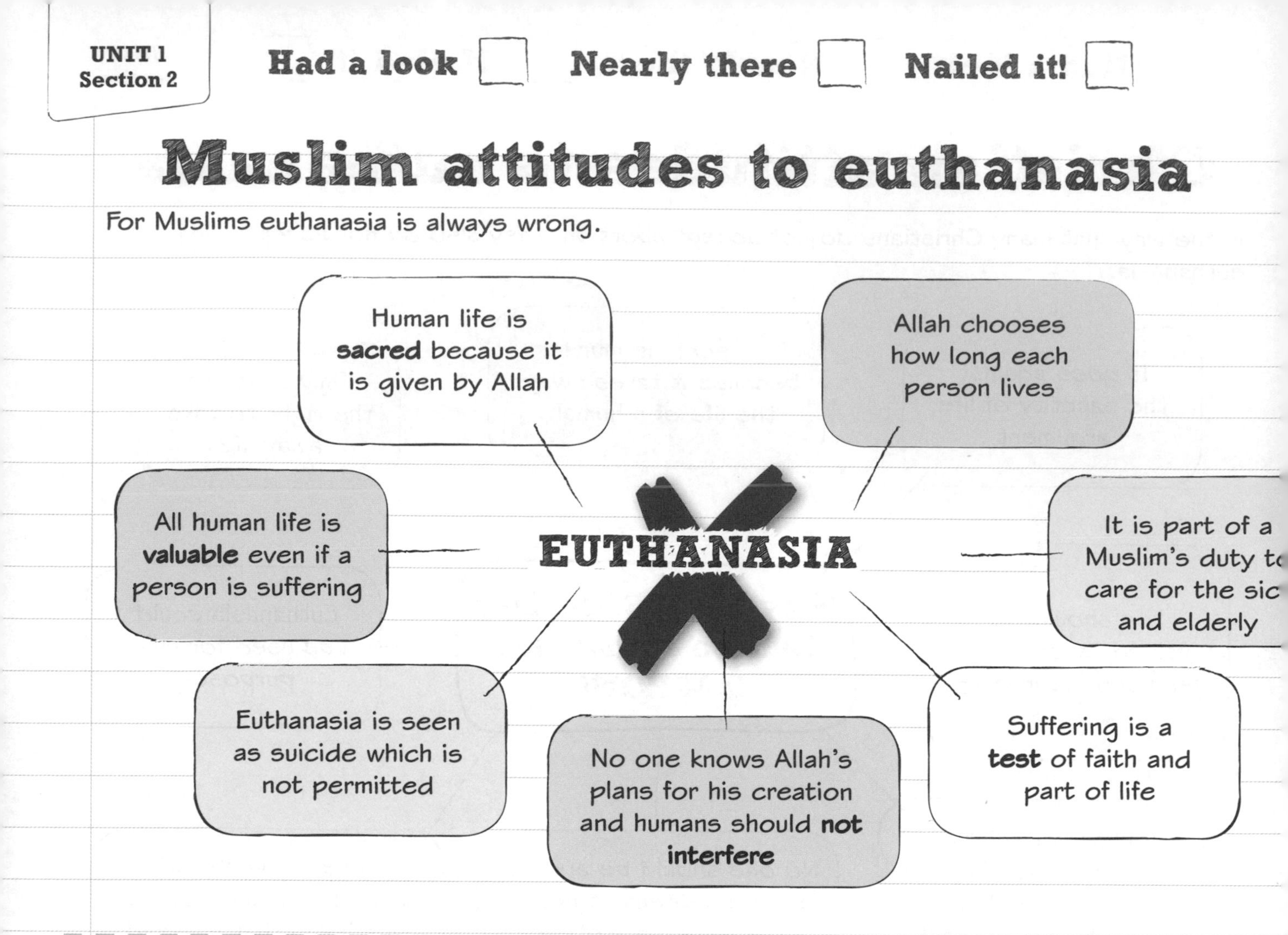

Why it is wrong

Euthanasia is seen as **wrong** like murder and suicide. Muslims believe they should trust their lives to Allah and life is a test which determines their afterlife. If they try to end their life, they may end up in Hell rather than paradise.

'No one dies unless God permits'. (3:145)

Is euthanasia ever right?

Some Muslims allow terminal patients to choose not to continue with medical treatment if it is causing hardship or family distress. Some Muslims would agree with turning off a life-support machine if nothing further can be done.

Now try this

1 Choose one religion other than Christianity and explain why some of its followers believe euthanasia is wrong. **(c, 8 marks)**

2 'Religious believers should always oppose euthanasia.' You should refer to at least one religion in your answer.

(i) Do you agree? Give reasons for your opinion. **(d, 3 marks)**

(ii) Give reasons why some people may disagree with you. **(3 marks)**

Matters of life and death in the media

There are many examples of how the media portrays matters of life and death. Make sure you can give arguments both for and against the media being free to criticise these ideas.

It's important that issues such as abortion are discussed in the media because:

- they affect everyone
- people hold strong opinions and it is important to be aware of different views
- they are controversial with many different views
- there are developments and the law may change which people need to know about.

Should the media criticise religious views on these issues?

FOR

- A variety of views are held and no view should be exempt.
- Religious views may be wrong or seen as out of date.
- It is important to debate views because they are constantly changing.

AGAINST

- Religious views should be respected as they've been around for a long time.
- They are based on traditional teachings such as those in the Bible.
- The media should present a range of ideas but not criticise them.

The media presents issues to the public through:

Newspapers Show opinions and highlight changes in law	**Internet** Makes news and views available but is not checked for accuracy	**Radio** Features or discussions on life and death issues	**Television news** Informs people on issues
Television documentaries Factual focus on life and death issues	**Soap operas** Storylines deal with difficult issues, which viewers can relate to	**Television dramas** Similar to soap operas	**Situation comedies** Use everyday situations for comedy but also deal with issues
Cartoons Deal with issues in a more light-hearted way		**Films** Many look at life and death issues in depth	

1 Do you think the media should criticise what religions say about life after death? Give two reasons for your opinion. **(b, 4 marks)**

Be sure to read the questions carefully. This question asks you to bring **two** topic ideas together – the media and life after death.

Had a look ☐ Nearly there ☐ Nailed it! ☐

Key words

It is important that you learn the key words for each topic. This is so you can explain what they mean for (a) type questions and use the key words in your answers to other questions to explain ideas fully.

Key words	Definitions
abortion	the removal of a foetus from the womb before it can survive
assisted suicide	providing a seriously ill person with the means to commit suicide
euthanasia	the painless killing of someone dying from a painful disease
immortality of the soul	the idea that the soul lives on after the death of the body
near-death experience	when someone about to die has an out of body experience
non-voluntary euthanasia	ending someone's life painlessly when they are unable to ask, but you have good reason for thinking they would want you to do so
paranormal	unexplained things which are thought to have spiritual causes e.g. ghosts, mediums
quality of life	the idea that life must have some benefits for it to be worth living
reincarnation	the belief that, after death, souls are reborn into a new body
resurrection	the belief that, after death, the body stays in the grave until the end of the world when it is raised
sanctity of life	the belief that life is holy and belongs to God
voluntary euthanasia	ending life painlessly when someone in great pain asks for death

Changing attitudes towards marriage and the family in the UK

Recently, attitudes towards issues such as marriage, divorce, the family and homosexuality have **changed** and you need to be aware of the reasons for this.

Reasons for change

- The UK is now a multi-faith and multi-ethnic society.
- People are more **tolerant** of difference.
- Less focus on Christian teachings.
- The Church has less influence.
- Decline in traditional family values.
- Women are more equal to men in society.
- Fewer people are getting married and more are choosing to cohabit (live together without being married).
- Fewer religious marriage ceremonies.
- Homosexuality is more acceptable (in the past it was a criminal offence).
- Civil Partnership Act 2004 allows same sex couples to have a legal commitment.

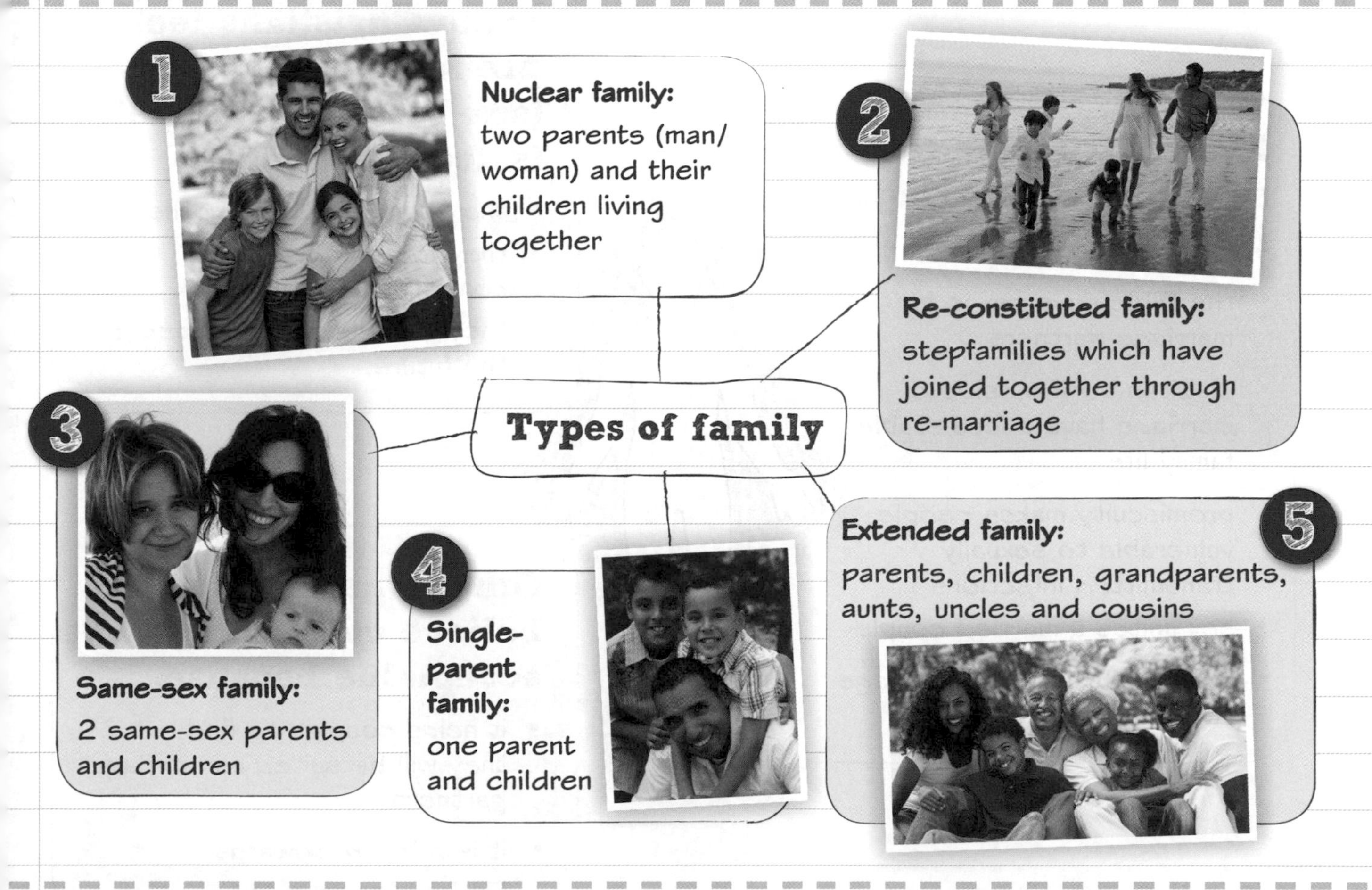

Now try this

1 What is **cohabitation**? (a, 2 marks)
2 What is **homosexuality**? (a, 2 marks)
3 Do you think attitudes to marriage have changed in the UK? Give two reasons for your point of view. (b, 4 marks)

Make sure you learn your key words thoroughly to help you do well on two-mark (a) questions.

Had a look ☐ Nearly there ☐ Nailed it! ☐

Christian attitudes to sex outside marriage

Most Christians believe that their religion teaches that sex outside marriage is wrong.

The Bible teaches:

- casual relationships are wrong
- sex is **special** and should be saved for marriage
- adultery is **forbidden** in the Ten Commandments
- married couples should be faithful to each other.

'You shall not commit adultery'.

(Exodus 20:14)

'God wants you to be holy and completely free from sexual immorality'.

(1 Thessalonians 4:3)

'Do you not know that your body is a temple of the Holy Spirit?'

(1 Corinthians 6:19)

Christian views

Most Christians feel sex outside marriage is wrong because:

- the Bible says sex is for marriage partners
- children born outside of marriage have a less stable family life
- promiscuity makes people vulnerable to sexually transmitted infections
- sex unites a married couple
- adultery breaks the marriage vows made before God.

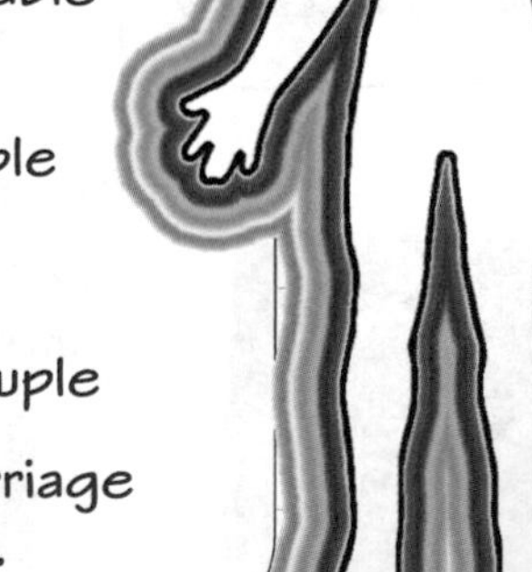

Some Christians feel pre-marital sex (sex before marriage) is acceptable if:

- the couple love each other
- they are in a long-term committed relationship
- they intend to get married in the future.

Other Christians believe cohabitation is acceptable because:

- it helps couples to find out if they will be suited as marriage partners
- it is a 'step' towards marriage.

Now try this

1 What is meant by **promiscuity**? **(a, 2 marks)**

2 Explain why most Christians are against sex outside marriage. **(c, 8 marks)**

Muslim attitudes to sex outside marriage

Sex outside marriage is strictly forbidden in Islam.

Islam teaches:

1. Sex should be kept **special** for marriage so at puberty boys and girls are kept separate.
2. Adultery is a sin and **forbidden** by Allah.
3. Muslims should not behave in a sexual manner towards others.
4. The main purpose of sex is procreation (to have children).
5. The ideal marriage partner is one who loves Allah.

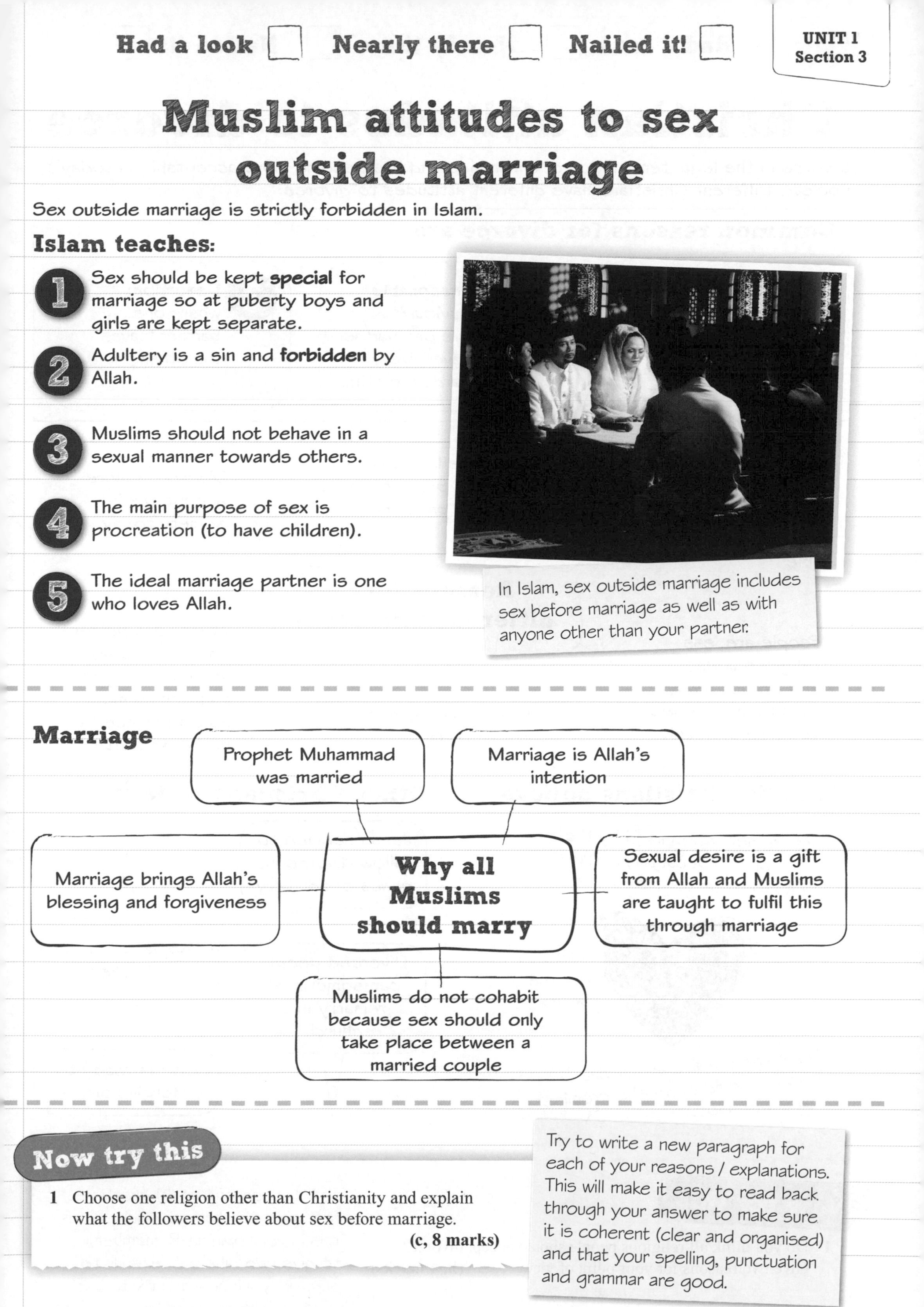

In Islam, sex outside marriage includes sex before marriage as well as with anyone other than your partner.

Marriage

Why all Muslims should marry

- Prophet Muhammad was married
- Marriage is Allah's intention
- Marriage brings Allah's blessing and forgiveness
- Sexual desire is a gift from Allah and Muslims are taught to fulfil this through marriage
- Muslims do not cohabit because sex should only take place between a married couple

Now try this

1 Choose one religion other than Christianity and explain what the followers believe about sex before marriage.

(c, 8 marks)

Try to write a new paragraph for each of your reasons / explanations. This will make it easy to read back through your answer to make sure it is coherent (clear and organised) and that your spelling, punctuation and grammar are good.

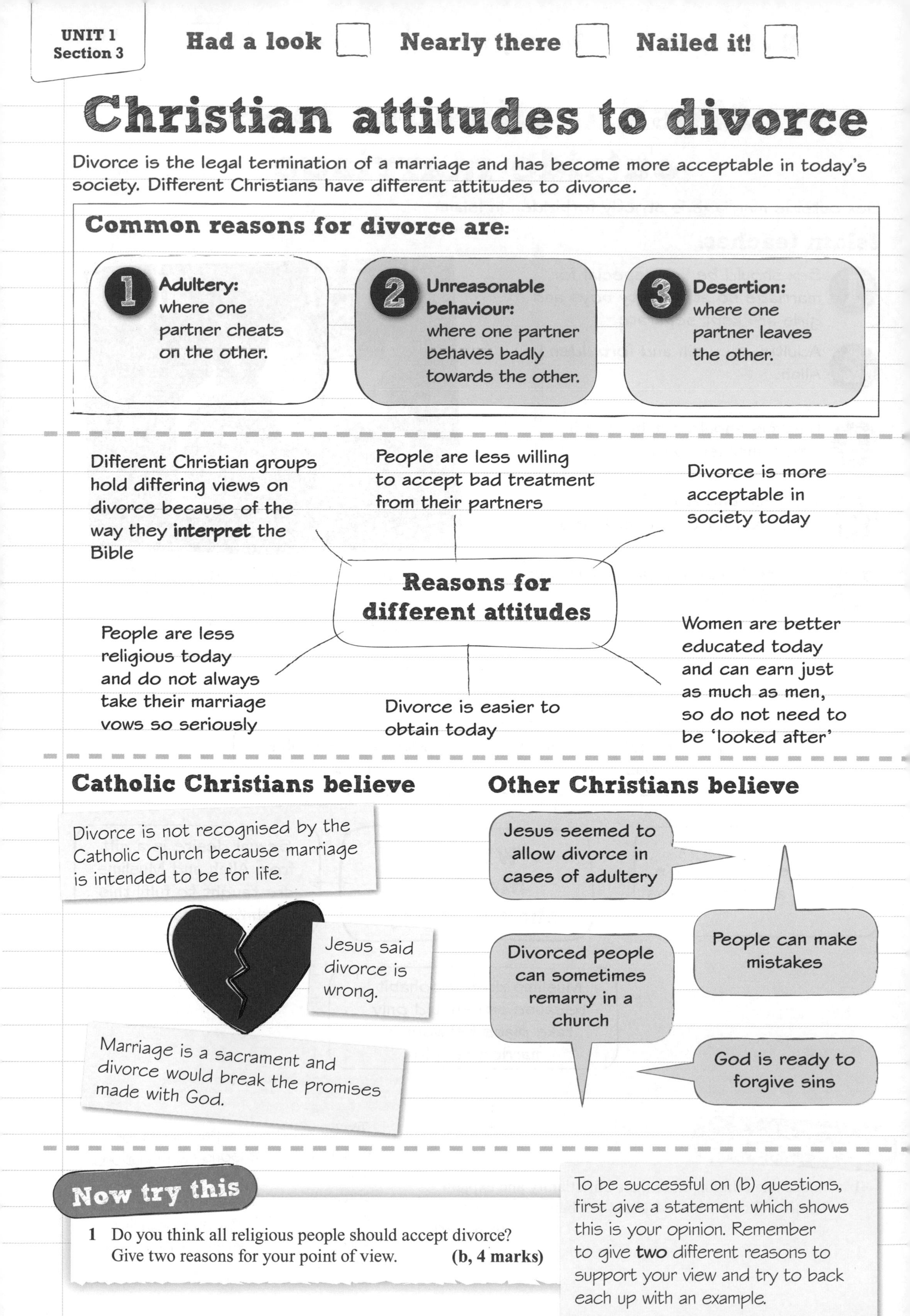

Christian attitudes to divorce

Divorce is the legal termination of a marriage and has become more acceptable in today's society. Different Christians have different attitudes to divorce.

Common reasons for divorce are:

1. **Adultery:** where one partner cheats on the other.
2. **Unreasonable behaviour:** where one partner behaves badly towards the other.
3. **Desertion:** where one partner leaves the other.

Reasons for different attitudes

- Different Christian groups hold differing views on divorce because of the way they **interpret** the Bible
- People are less willing to accept bad treatment from their partners
- Divorce is more acceptable in society today
- People are less religious today and do not always take their marriage vows so seriously
- Divorce is easier to obtain today
- Women are better educated today and can earn just as much as men, so do not need to be 'looked after'

Catholic Christians believe

Divorce is not recognised by the Catholic Church because marriage is intended to be for life.

Jesus said divorce is wrong.

Marriage is a sacrament and divorce would break the promises made with God.

Other Christians believe

Jesus seemed to allow divorce in cases of adultery

People can make mistakes

Divorced people can sometimes remarry in a church

God is ready to forgive sins

Now try this

1 Do you think all religious people should accept divorce? Give two reasons for your point of view. **(b, 4 marks)**

To be successful on (b) questions, first give a statement which shows this is your opinion. Remember to give **two** different reasons to support your view and try to back each up with an example.

Muslim attitudes to divorce

In Islam, marriage is a contract which means Muslims can legally get divorced. However, although it is allowed, Muslims do not like divorce and it is a **last resort**.

Divorce in Islam

1 The husband must announce his intention to divorce his wife three times over a period of three months

2 During this time the couple live together but do not have sex to avoid pregnancy

The couple and their families have a chance to try and work things out

After three months has passed, the couple are free to remarry

Different Muslim attitudes to divorce

Most Muslims accept divorce (as a last resort) because:

✔ Marriage is a contract in Islam, not a promise to Allah.

✔ The Qur'an allows Muslims to divorce.

✔ Islam has rules for how divorce is to happen and how divorced women and children are to be cared for.

✔ The family is very important to Muslims and they feel it may be better for children to have divorced parents than to live with hatred and bitterness.

Others do not because:

✘ Muhammad, the perfect example, did not divorce.

✘ Muhammad said divorce was the most hated of all things that Allah has permitted.

✘ Divorce may damage the lives of the children.

✘ Divorce shows disrespect to the family.

Last resorts

As a last resort Muslim women may divorce their husbands if the husband:

- is absent for a long period of time
- is in prison
- refuses to provide for the wife
- is unable to have sex.

Now try this

1 Chose one religion other than Christianity and explain why some of the followers accept divorce and others do not. **(c, 8 marks)**

Christian teachings on family life

The family unit and family life are very important to Christians.

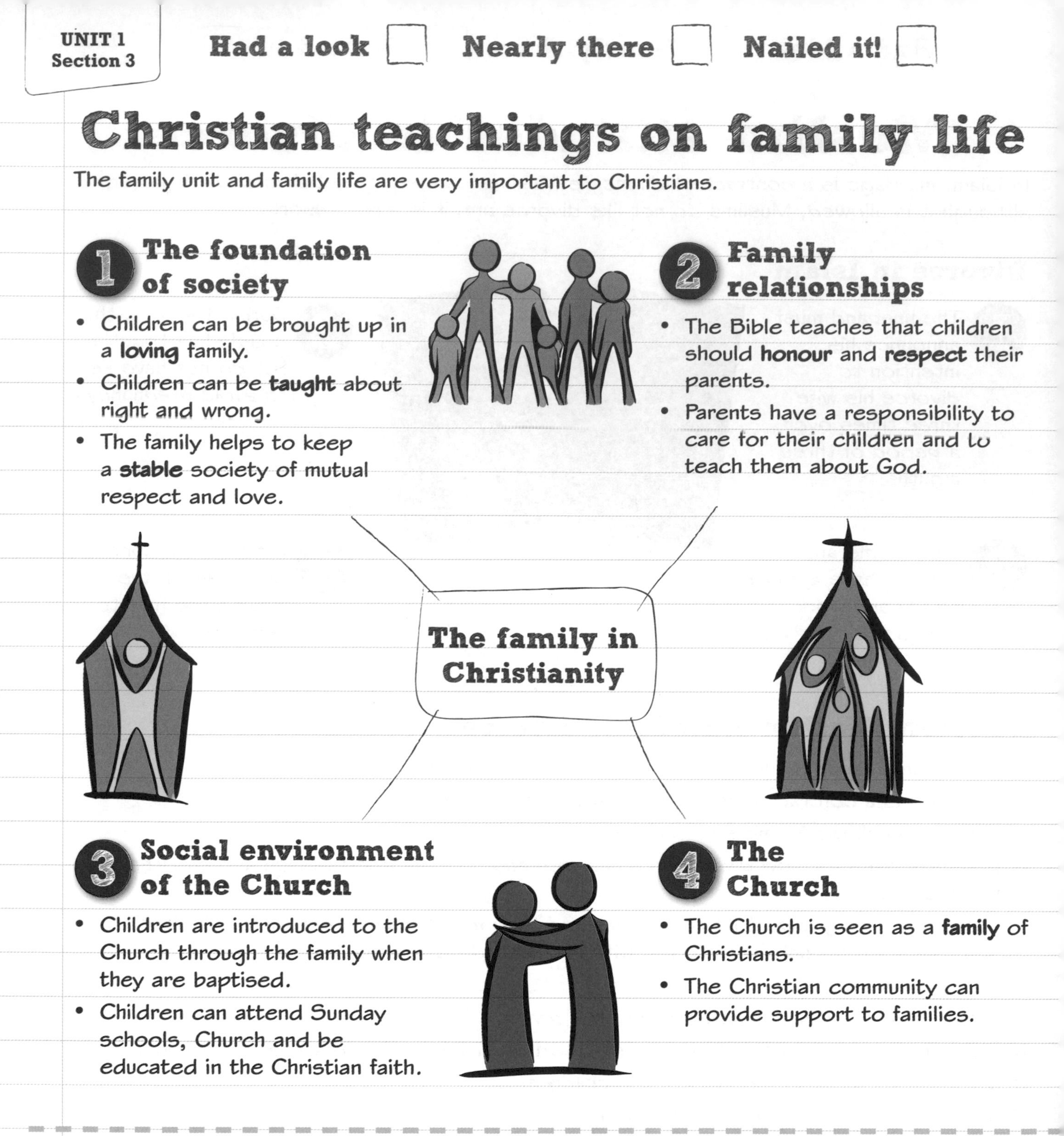

The family in Christianity

1 The foundation of society

- Children can be brought up in a **loving** family.
- Children can be **taught** about right and wrong.
- The family helps to keep a **stable** society of mutual respect and love.

2 Family relationships

- The Bible teaches that children should **honour** and **respect** their parents.
- Parents have a responsibility to care for their children and to teach them about God.

3 Social environment of the Church

- Children are introduced to the Church through the family when they are baptised.
- Children can attend Sunday schools, Church and be educated in the Christian faith.

4 The Church

- The Church is seen as a **family** of Christians.
- The Christian community can provide support to families.

Now try this

1 Do you think family life is important? Give two reasons to support your point of view. **(b, 4 marks)**

2 'Families are the best place to bring up children'.
In your answer you should refer to at least one religion.

(i) Do you agree? Give reasons for your opinion. **(d, 3 marks)**

(ii) Give reasons why some people may disagree with you. **(3 marks)**

Use the information above to help you answer this question. Remember to support your opinion with two valid and relevant reasons.

Spend time reading the statement in a (d) question to make sure you properly understand it, and therefore what you need to write. Also, try to give at least one religious reason.

Muslim teachings on family life

The family is very important in Islam.

The traditional Muslim family

- Traditionally, Muslim families are extended families. They include parents, children, grandparents and other relatives.
- Muslims believe extended families offer greater stability, love and support.
- The elderly are treated with respect and children are expected to look after older family members.
- It is at the heart of the community.

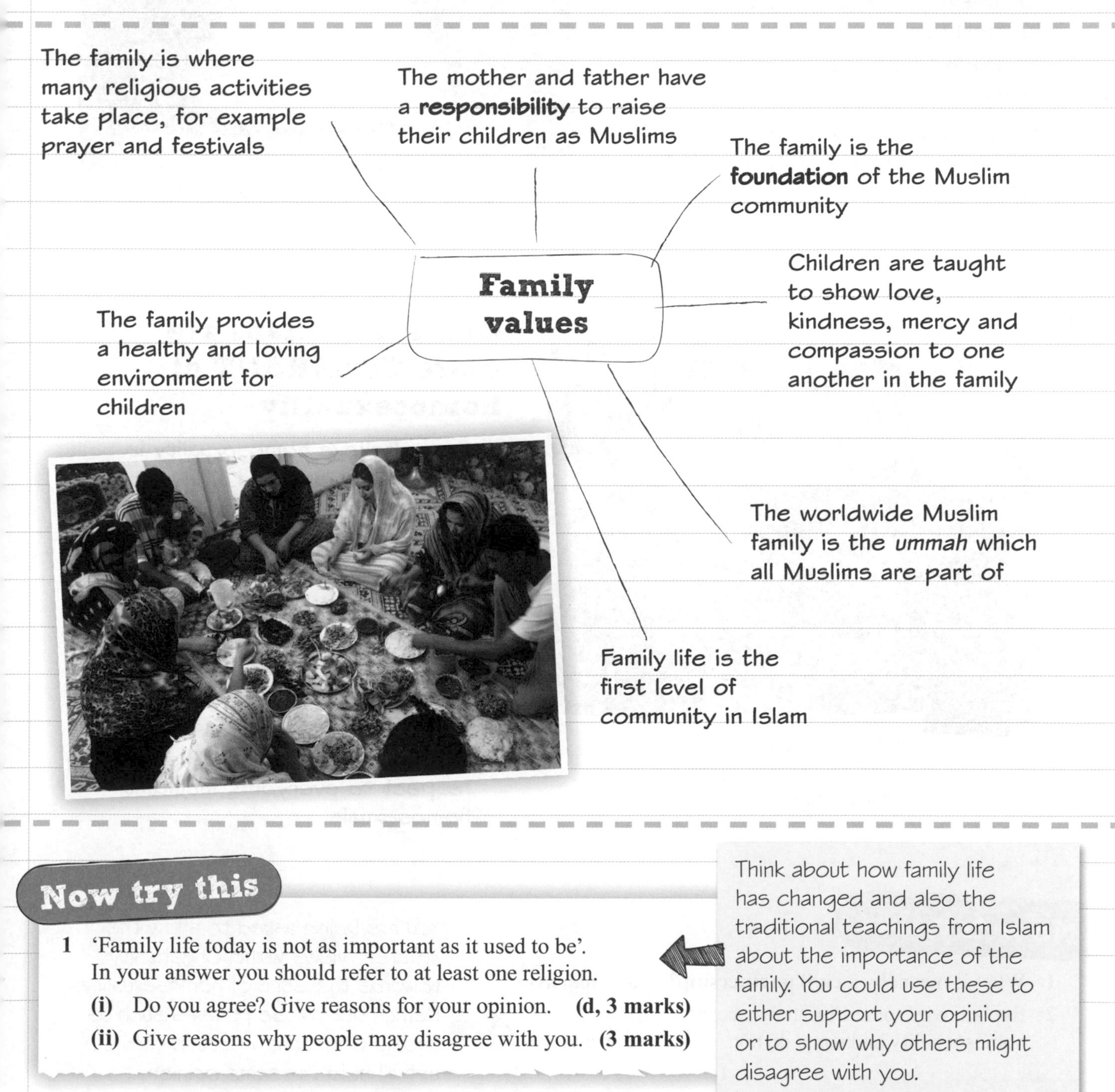

Now try this

1 'Family life today is not as important as it used to be'.
In your answer you should refer to at least one religion.

(i) Do you agree? Give reasons for your opinion. **(d, 3 marks)**

(ii) Give reasons why people may disagree with you. **(3 marks)**

Think about how family life has changed and also the traditional teachings from Islam about the importance of the family. You could use these to either support your opinion or to show why others might disagree with you.

Had a look ☐ Nearly there ☐ Nailed it! ☐

Christian attitudes to homosexuality

Christians are divided over their views on the topic of homosexuality.

Some Christians believe homosexuality is WRONG because

- Marriage was intended by God to be between one man and one woman.
- Same-sex partners cannot have **children** naturally which is a purpose of Christian marriage.
- Homosexuality is seen to undermine the family unit.
- The Bible teaches homosexuality is wrong.
- Some Christians teach that homosexuals should remain celibate (never have sex).

Most Christians traditionally believe and teach that marriage should be for one man and one woman.

In some Churches, there is more tolerance for same-sex relationships

Other Christians are more TOLERANT of homosexuality

- Some believe homosexuality is perfectly **natural** and all humans are created equal by God.
- Some Christians will bless a homosexual civil partnership.
- Same-sex couples demonstrate feelings such as love for each other so should be allowed to celebrate their commitment.
- Jesus taught Christians to 'love thy neighbour'. This means showing **respect** to everyone, including homosexuals.

Now try this

1. What is meant by a **civil partnership**? **(a, 2 marks)**
2. Explain why some Christians accept homosexuality and some do not. **(c, 8 marks)**

You are being asked to show the different views within Christianity towards the issue of homosexuality. Remember to use phrases such as 'Some Christians' because they do not all hold the same opinions.

Muslim attitudes to homosexuality

Most Muslims strongly oppose homosexuality and do not believe it should be permitted.

Muslim beliefs

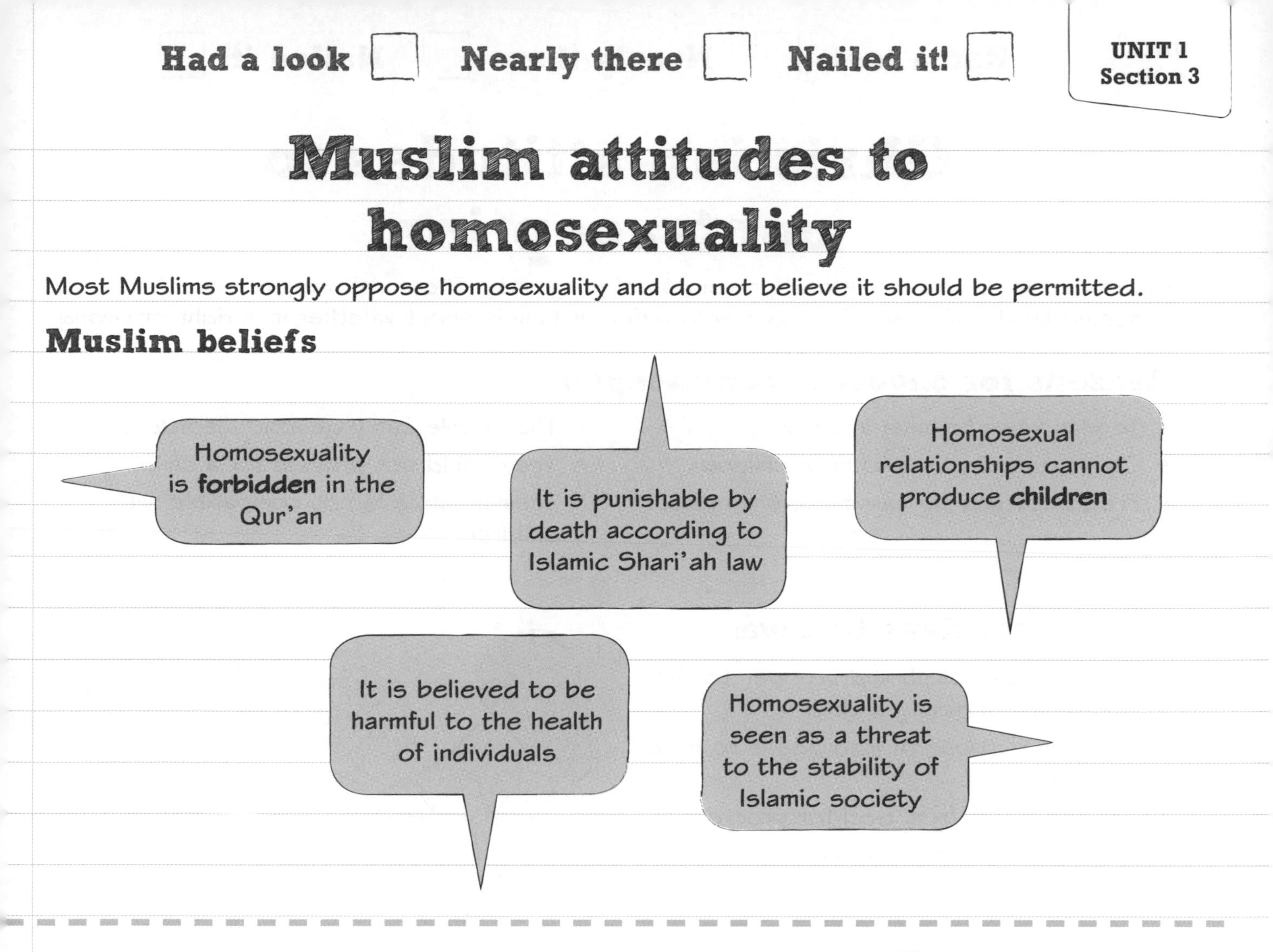

Alternative views

Islam traditionally teaches that homosexuality is a chosen not natural sexual orientation. However, some modern Muslims offer support to other Muslims who believe they are homosexual so that they are not excluded from the Muslim community.

Some Muslims will also accept the scientific evidence that suggests that homosexuality is not a choice.

EXAM ALERT!

When answering (c) type questions on **one religion other than Christianity**, make sure that you really focus on this religion and don't include any reference to Christianity. Try to include references to sacred texts to support your answer.

Students have struggled with this topic in recent exams – **be prepared!** ResultsPlus

The media

Issues surrounding being a Muslim and being gay have been discussed in the media in cases such as the Masood family in *EastEnders* but still many claim that it is impossible to be both. For many Muslims, laws against homosexuality cannot be changed.

Now try this

1 Choose one religion other than Christianity and explain why some of its followers are against homosexuality. **(c, 8 marks)**

Remember that this question is worth 8 marks so aim to **explain fully** why Muslims do not accept homosexuality. Try to include reference to the Qur'an and Shari'ah law.

Had a look ☐ Nearly there ☐ Nailed it! ☐

Christian attitudes to contraception

Contraception is the intentional prevention of pregnancy. There are many reasons for choosing to do this, and Christians hold different beliefs about whether it is right or wrong.

Reasons for choosing contraception

- To plan when to have a family.
- They are too young to have children.
- Pregnancy may be harmful to the mother.
- The couple carry genetic disorders.
- They could not provide for a child.
- Their lifestyle is not compatible with children.

Some Christians believe:

- every sexual act should be open to the possibility of having a child
- the main purpose of marriage is to have children
- sex was a gift from God for procreation
- contraception may encourage promiscuity.

Some Christians believe every sperm is sacred and every sexual act should be open to having a child.

Other Christians believe:

Using contraception is **not** a sin

Contraception can be used to help family planning

In times of financial difficulty or ill health, contraception may be more acceptable

Sex is not just for procreation

Some other Christians believe that sex is not just for procreation but also for pleasure and using contraception is sensible.

Now try this

1 What is **contraception**? **(a, 2 marks)**

2 Do you think it is irresponsible not to use contraception? Give two reasons for your opinion. **(b, 4 marks)**

Muslim attitudes to contraception

Muslims are **divided** on their views about contraception. As there is no specific reference in the Qur'an to contraception, different groups approach the use of it differently and have different attitudes to it.

Some Muslims **oppose** the use of contraception.

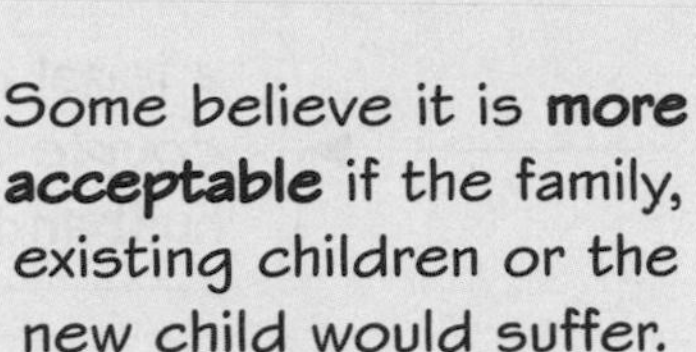

Some believe it is **more acceptable** if the family, existing children or the new child would suffer.

Others argue it is **acceptable** where the life or health of the mother is put at risk.

Acceptable

- Muslim authorities allow the use of contraception to preserve the life of the mother.
- Some believe Muhammad supported the withdrawal method of contraception.
- In some Muslim countries, contraception is taught through leaflets and posters for economic reasons.
- Some suggest that all non-permanent methods of contraception are acceptable for married couples.
- Both partners should be married and should consent to the type of contraception used.

Not acceptable

- In strict Muslim countries only natural forms of contraception are allowed.
- Permanent methods (vasectomy or sterilisation) are forbidden.
- Methods that cause an early abortion are not acceptable.
- Having children is very important in Muslim families and the use of contraception would prevent this, so it is discouraged.

Now try this

1 Do you agree with the use of contraception? Give two reasons for your opinion. **(b, 4 marks)**

2 Choose one religion other than Christianity and explain why some of its followers accept contraception and others do not. **(c, 8 marks)**

Had a look ☐ Nearly there ☐ Nailed it! ☐

Key words

It is important that you learn the key words for each topic. This is so you can explain what they mean for (a) type questions and use the key words in your answers to other questions to explain ideas fully.

Key words	Definitions
adultery	a sexual act between a married person and someone other than their marriage partner
civil partnership	a legal ceremony giving a homosexual couple the same legal rights as a husband and wife
cohabitation	living together without being married
contraception	intentionally preventing pregnancy from occurring
faithfulness	staying with your marriage partner and having sex only with them
homosexuality	sexual attraction to the same sex
nuclear family	mother, father and children living as a unit
pre-marital sex	sex before marriage
procreation	making a new life
promiscuity	having sex with a number of partners without commitment
re-constituted family	where two sets of children (stepbrothers and stepsisters) become one family when their divorced parents marry each other
re-marriage	marrying again after being divorced from a previous marriage

Changing attitudes to gender roles in the UK

The roles of men and women have **changed** significantly over the past 100 years.

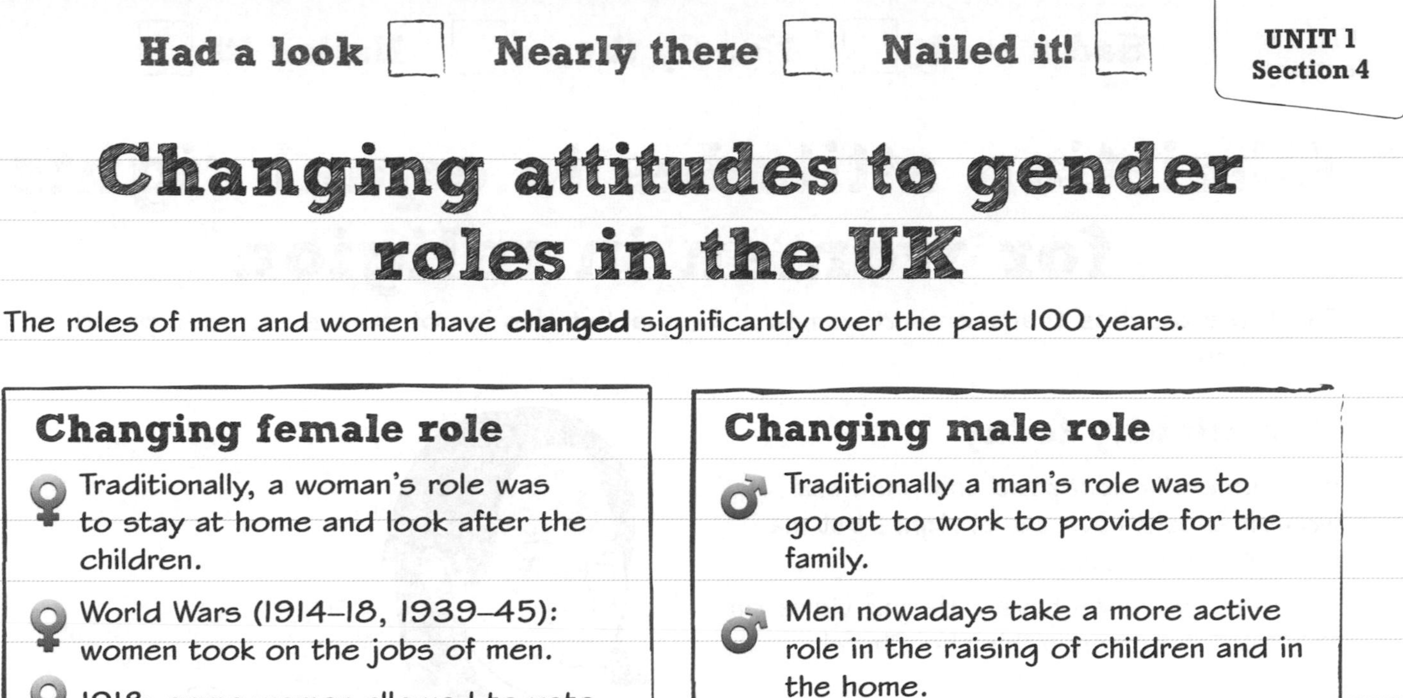

Changing female role

- Traditionally, a woman's role was to stay at home and look after the children.
- World Wars (1914–18, 1939–45): women took on the jobs of men.
- 1918: some women allowed to vote.
- 1945: post-war, many women wanted equality and an end to sexism.
- 1970: women given rights to equal pay.

Changing male role

- Traditionally a man's role was to go out to work to provide for the family.
- Men nowadays take a more active role in the raising of children and in the home.
- Men are willing to do tasks traditionally seen as 'women's work' such as cooking.

How roles have changed		Why roles have changed
Women can vote and become MPs.	→	Changes in the law.
Women can do any job they want.	→	Change in the law, effect of wars.
Women are better educated.	→	Effective contraception, equal rights legislation.
Men are more involved in childcare and home-life.	→	Changes in attitudes.

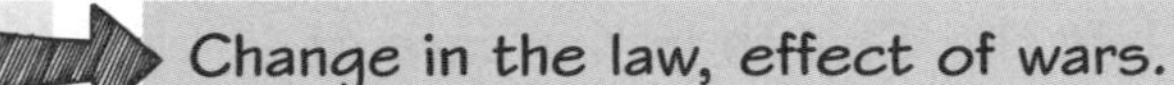

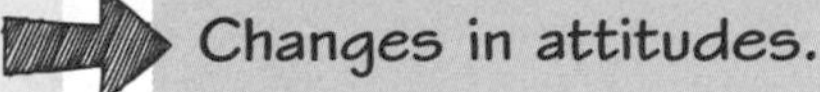

Are male and female roles now equal?

- Men and women have equal rights and women are achieving success in all areas.
- **But** inequalities still exist: roles such as nursing are still seen as female.
- Girls are achieving higher grades in examinations.
- **But** surveys show that men can still earn 17% more than women for the same job.
- **Why?** Many blame it on women having career breaks to have children. Some blame discrimination or prejudice.

Now try this

1. What is meant by **sexism**? **(a, 2 marks)**
2. Explain how attitudes towards the roles of men and women have changed in the UK. **(c, 8 marks)**

The word 'explain' is used in this question so try to make sure you show how the roles have changed and give examples to illustrate what you mean rather than just list the changes.

Had a look ☐ Nearly there ☐ Nailed it! ☐

Christian attitudes to equal rights for women in religion

The Bible teaches that men and women are equal but this is not always shown in practice in religion.

Christianity today

It is generally accepted that men and women should have **equal rights** but may have **different** roles.

Different churches have differing views on the role of women within the Church.

Some Churches allow female priests but others do not.

Reasons NOT to accept women as Church leaders

- ✗ The Bible says women should obey their husbands.
- ✗ The Bible says women should be silent in Church.
- ✗ All of Jesus' disciples were men.
- ✗ Jesus left the Church in the care of St Peter and he was a man.
- ✗ In the past women were regarded as inferior because of Adam and Eve (Eve was sinful).

Reasons to ACCEPT women as Church leaders

- ✔ The Bible says 'God created men and women in his own image'.
- ✔ Jesus did **not** discriminate between men and women; he talked to and taught both.
- ✔ Women followers were treated well by Jesus and it was women who stayed by his cross and were first to see him after the resurrection.
- ✔ There is evidence of women leaders in the early Church.
- ✔ The Golden Rule suggests that everyone should be respected.

Different ways of interpreting the Bible

There are differences of opinion about the roles of women in religion because of the different ways Christians interpret the Bible.

- Some Christians believe that the Bible is the absolute word of God so anything it says cannot be changed or avoided. It must be taken literally.
- Some Christians believe the Bible was written down by humans and reflects the view of people at that time.
- Other Christians believe the Bible is relevant as a moral guideline but has to be changed and adapted for today's society.

Now try this

1 Do you think women should have the same religious rights as men? Give two reasons for your point of view. **(b, 4 marks)**

Remember to give **two** different reasons for your opinion, perhaps giving examples of religious beliefs or teachings in your answer.

Muslim attitudes to equal rights for women

Muslims believe that Allah created all humans **equal** but **not the same**. They are seen to have different roles and responsibilities.

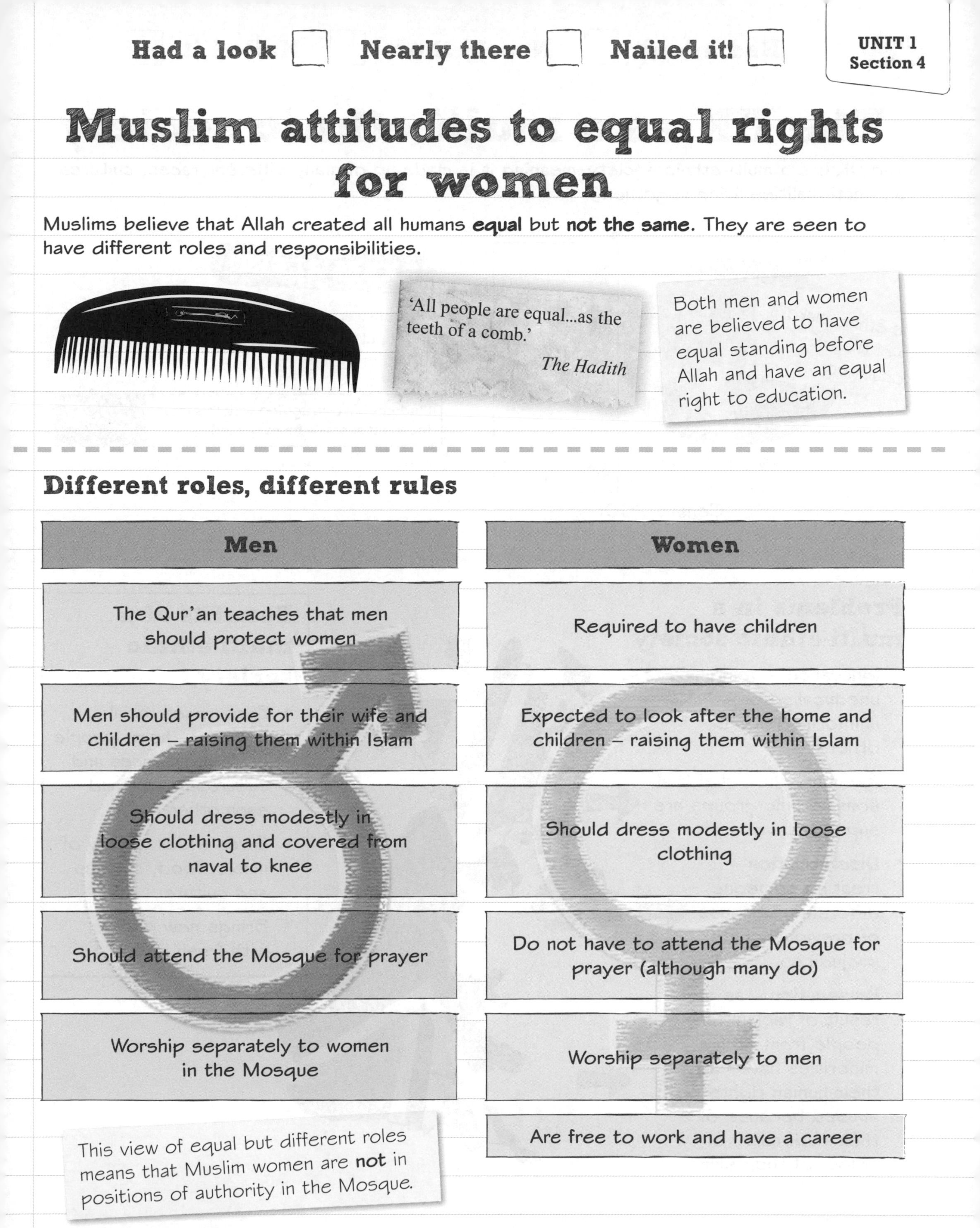

'All people are equal...as the teeth of a comb.'

The Hadith

Both men and women are believed to have equal standing before Allah and have an equal right to education.

Different roles, different rules

Men	Women
The Qur'an teaches that men should protect women	Required to have children
Men should provide for their wife and children – raising them within Islam	Expected to look after the home and children – raising them within Islam
Should dress modestly in loose clothing and covered from naval to knee	Should dress modestly in loose clothing
Should attend the Mosque for prayer	Do not have to attend the Mosque for prayer (although many do)
Worship separately to women in the Mosque	Worship separately to men
	Are free to work and have a career

This view of equal but different roles means that Muslim women are **not** in positions of authority in the Mosque.

Now try this

1 Do you think men and women are treated equally in religion? Give two reasons for your point of view. **(b, 4 marks)**

You could try to answer this with reference to Islam. It is also worth beginning your answer with a statement to show that this is your own opinion.

The UK as a multi-ethnic society

The UK has a multi-ethnic society, meaning it is made up of many different races, cultures and nationalities living together.

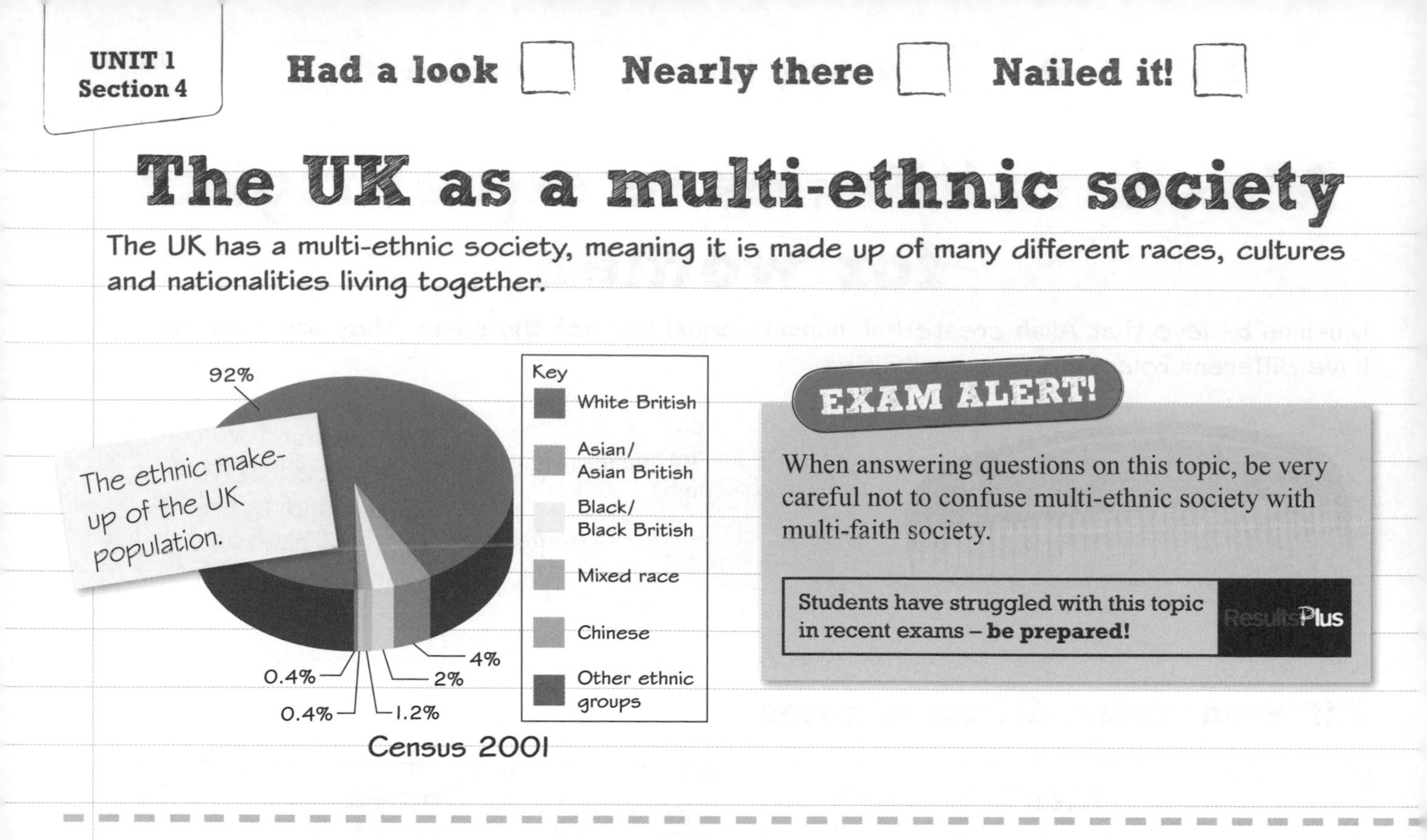

The ethnic make-up of the UK population.

EXAM ALERT!

When answering questions on this topic, be very careful not to confuse multi-ethnic society with multi-faith society.

Students have struggled with this topic in recent exams – **be prepared!** ResultsPlus

Problems in a multi-ethnic society

- **Ignorance** – being uneducated or uninformed about others.
- **Racism** – the belief that some ethnic groups are superior to others.
- **Discrimination** – treating someone differently because of previously held prejudices.
- **Persecution** – as a result of racism, many people from ethnic minorities have had their human rights abused because of their nationality or colour of their skin.

Benefits of a multi-ethnic society

- Encourages racial harmony – helps people of different races and cultures understand each other.
- Gives wider variety of music, food, clothes and culture.
- Brings new people with fresh ideas.

Now try this

1 What is an **ethnic minority**? **(a, 2 marks)**
2 What is **racism**? **(a, 2 marks)**

Make sure you learn the key words to help you successfully answer (a) questions.

Government action to promote community cohesion

The UK has always offered a safe place for people from overseas who may be escaping troubles or trying to find work and improve their lives. The government has tried to encourage all people living in the UK to live and work together **peacefully**.

Different communities living together

Sharing a common vision and sense of belonging

Appreciating and valuing the differences between people

Community cohesion

Ensuring equal opportunities for all

Making strong and positive relationships between people

What has the Government done to prevent racial discrimination?

1. Race Relations Act 1976 – made it unlawful to discriminate because of race, colour, ethnic or national origin in employment, housing, education or welfare.
2. Made it illegal to use abusive or insulting words of a racial nature in public, or to publish articles that could stir up racism.
3. Commission for Racial Equality – established to fight racism, teach the importance of racial equality and deal with complaints of racism.
4. 'Britishness' test – all new immigrants to the UK must take the test to ensure they have a basic knowledge of British life.
5. The Community Facilitation Programme and Neighbourhood Renewal Units – set up to ensure ethnic minority communities had the skills necessary for work, opportunities for young people, appropriate healthcare and that their needs were met.

Now try this

1 What is **community cohesion**? **(a, 2 marks)**

2 Explain how the Government works to promote community cohesion in the UK. **(c, 8 marks)**

Make sure you read the question carefully. Here, for example, you are not asked to refer to a religion. Remember that you will be assessed on QWC in these questions so read back through your answer to make sure it is clear, organised and that your spelling, punctuation and grammar are good.

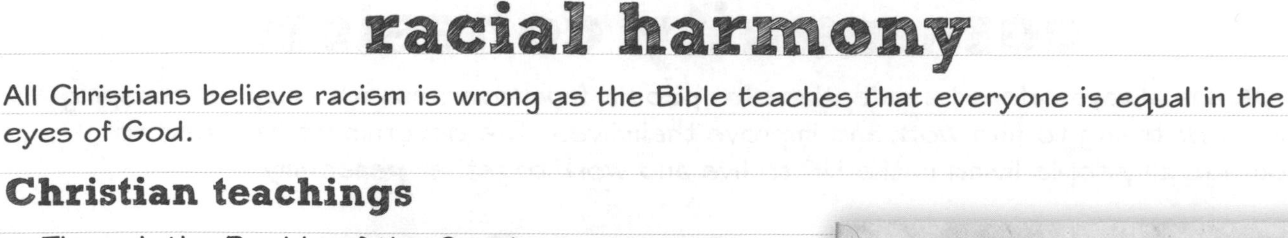

Why Christians should promote racial harmony

All Christians believe racism is wrong as the Bible teaches that everyone is equal in the eyes of God.

Christian teachings

- Through the Parable of the Good Samaritan Jesus taught that people follow God's command and **love** one another.

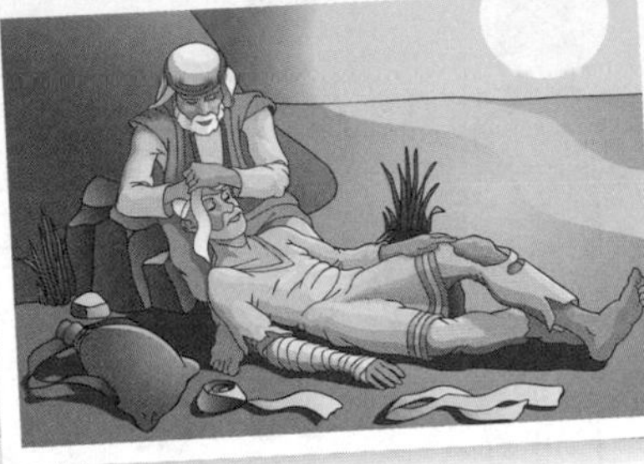

- The Golden Rule states 'Treat others the way you would like to be treated'.
- Christians believe they should promote **racial harmony** because through doing this they are putting these teachings into practice.

> For God created man in his own image. *Genesis 1:27*
>
> Love your neighbour as yourself. *Luke 10:27*

Racial harmony is when all races live together happily. The Bible teaches that all Christians are '**one people**'.

Examples

Dr Martin Luther King Jr (1929–1968)

- Worked for equality for black people in the USA.
- Put Christian principles of helping others and treating people equally into action.
- Thanks to his work black people were given equal voting rights in 1965.

Today

- Christian Churches condemn racism and encourage all Christians to treat everyone the same.
- In the UK the Church of England has its own Race and Community Relationships Committee. It advises Christians about issues of racism and helping racial minorities with issues of unemployment and imprisonment.

Now try this

1 'Christians should always promote racial harmony'.
In your answer you should refer to at least one religion.

(i) Do you agree? Give reasons for your opinion. **(d, 3 marks)**

(ii) Give reasons why some people may disagree with you. **(3 marks)**

2 Do you think religious people do enough to combat racism?
Give two reasons for your point of view. **(b, 4 marks)**

Remember to read the question carefully to make sure you understand what the question is asking. Also, you could try to support your reasons with examples.

Why Muslims should promote racial harmony

Islam teaches that all people are equal and therefore racism is always wrong. All Muslims are part of the *ummah* – the Islamic community of Muslims worldwide.

Reasons why Muslims promote racial harmony

Allah created all humans.

The Prophet declared in his last sermon that 'there is no difference between Arabs and non-Arabs'.

All Muslims are part of the *ummah* and come from every race in the world.

All races are loved by Allah.

The Qur'an teaches that **no** race is better than any other.

Prophet Muhammad declared that all people were descended from Adam and Eve.

Examples: How Muslims promote unity

1. Muslims pray together in Arabic.
2. Muslims from all over the world make the pilgrimage (*Hajj*) to the holy city.
3. All Muslims fast during the month of Ramadan.
4. All Muslims pray facing Makkah.

Malcolm X (1925–1965)

- African-American Muslim who campaigned for racial equality after his family was attacked.
- Became a minister for the radical Nation of Islam organisation and spread the message that a state should be established for black people alone.
- Believed *Hajj* was the greatest example of racial harmony.
- Continued to campaign for racial equality after leaving the Nation of Islam.

Now try this

1 Choose one religion other than Christianity and explain why its followers should work to promote racial harmony. **(c, 8 marks)**

Use your knowledge of Islam to answer this question remembering to fully develop the ideas you include.

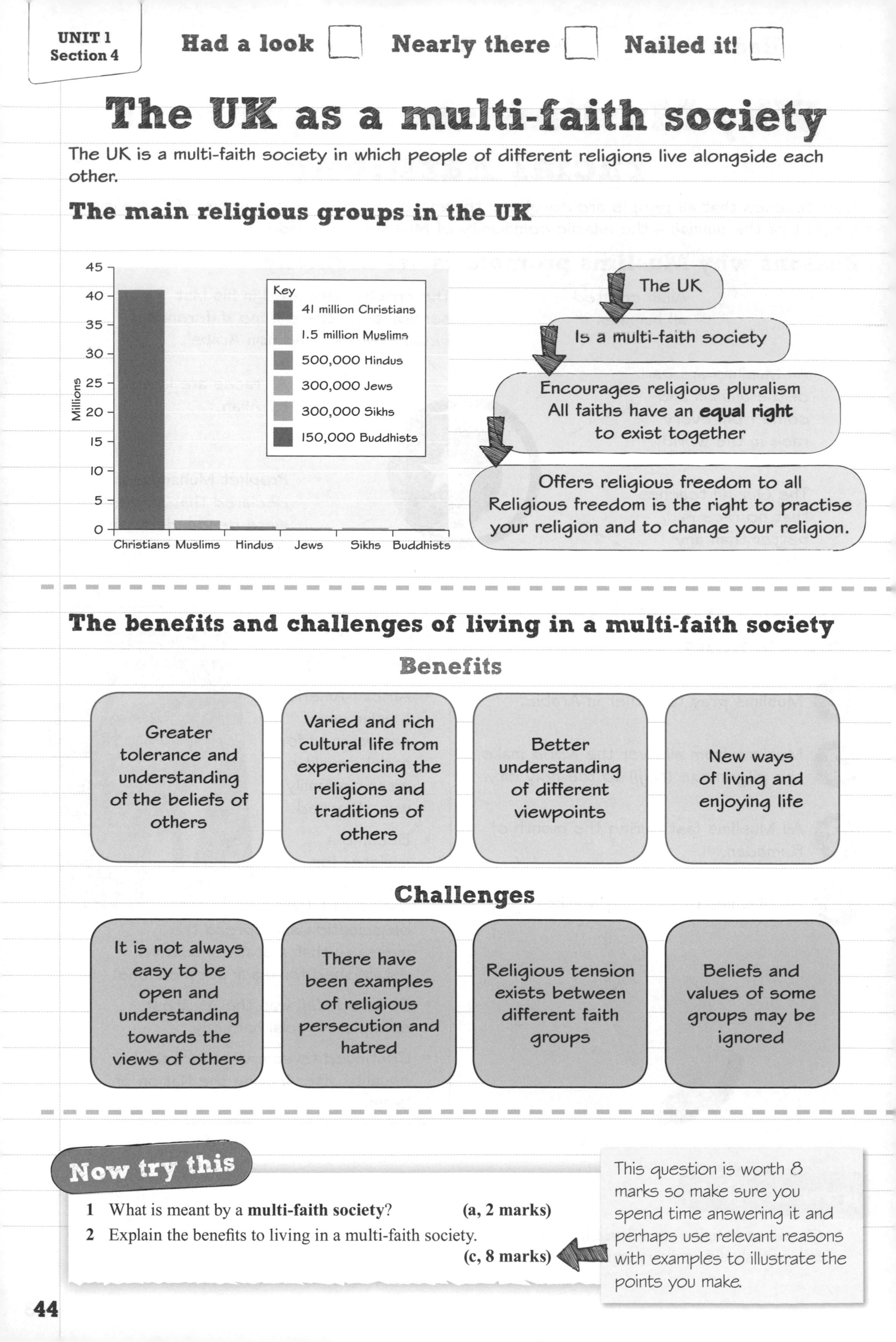

The UK as a multi-faith society

The UK is a multi-faith society in which people of different religions live alongside each other.

The main religious groups in the UK

The benefits and challenges of living in a multi-faith society

Benefits

- Greater tolerance and understanding of the beliefs of others
- Varied and rich cultural life from experiencing the religions and traditions of others
- Better understanding of different viewpoints
- New ways of living and enjoying life

Challenges

- It is not always easy to be open and understanding towards the views of others
- There have been examples of religious persecution and hatred
- Religious tension exists between different faith groups
- Beliefs and values of some groups may be ignored

Now try this

1. What is meant by a **multi-faith society**? **(a, 2 marks)**
2. Explain the benefits to living in a multi-faith society. **(c, 8 marks)**

This question is worth 8 marks so make sure you spend time answering it and perhaps use relevant reasons with examples to illustrate the points you make.

Issues raised about multi-faith societies

Different faiths existing alongside each other in a country can raise some important **issues**.

Viewpoints about a multi-faith society

Most religious believers in the UK believe that people should follow the religion of their choice. However, others do not agree.

God

Exclusivism only one religion is right and all others are wrong. Members of the 'right' faith should try to convert all others.

2 Inclusivism only one religion is completely right. Other religions may lead to God and should be respected but followers should be 'encouraged' to change faith.

3 Religious pluralism many different religions lead to God and each one should be fully respected and treated equally.

Conversion – there can be issues where one group of religious believers try to convert another to their faith, which could cause conflict.

Raising children within interfaith marriages – both parents may want their children raised within their own faith. A mixture of beliefs could lead to confusion.

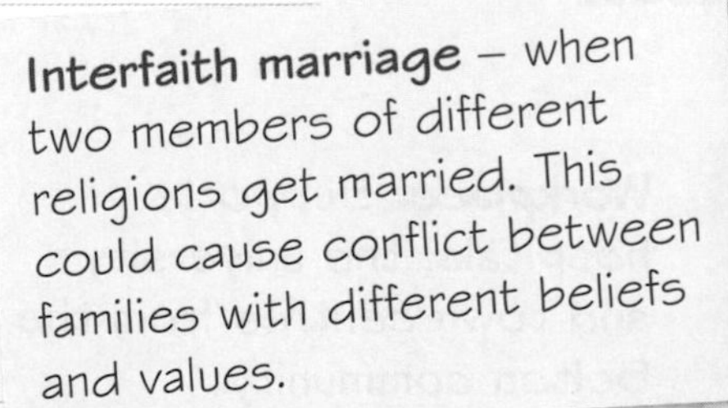

Now try this

1 What is meant by an **interfaith marriage**? **(a, 2 marks)**

2 'All religious people should try and convert others to their religion'. In your answer you should refer to at least one religion.

(i) Do you agree? Give reasons for your opinion. **(d, 3 marks)**

(ii) Give reasons why some people may disagree with you. **(3 marks)**

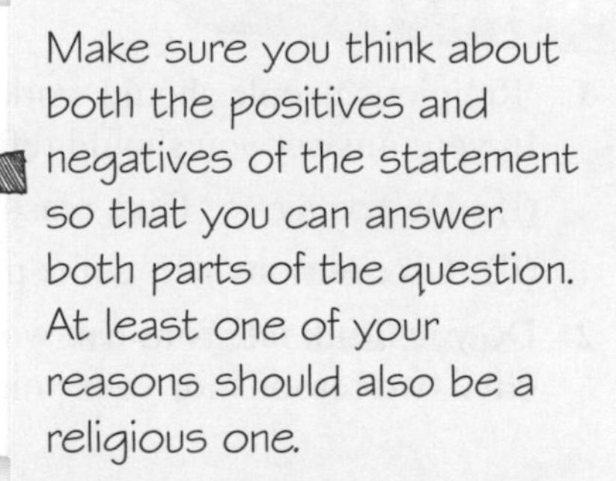

Had a look ☐ Nearly there ☐ Nailed it! ☐

Religion and community cohesion

Community cohesion is when all groups in society share a **common vision** and sense of belonging.

There are many organisations that try to establish community cohesion and better relationships between faiths in the UK. To live peacefully together they will need to:

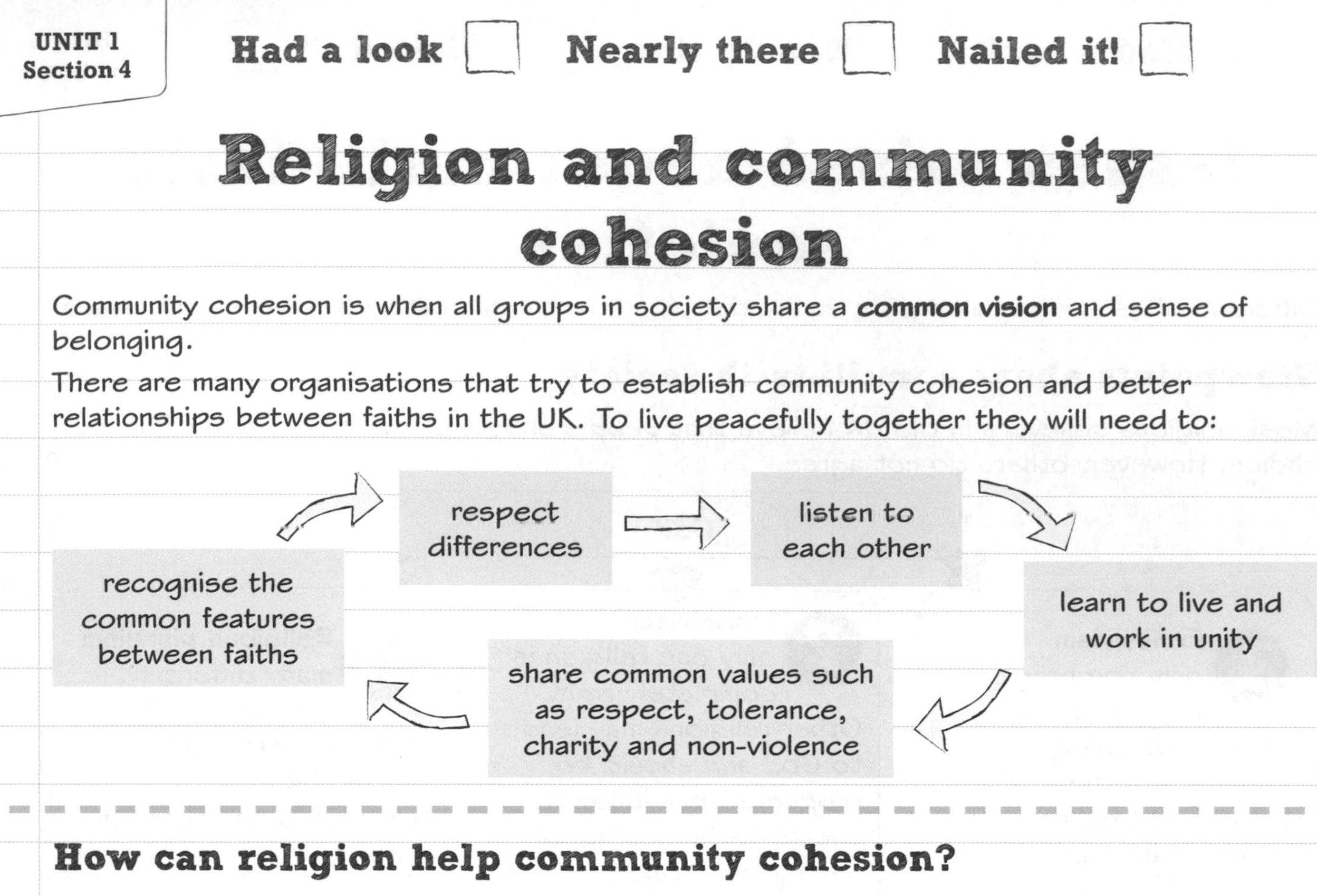

How can religion help community cohesion?

- Through religious groups, such as the Council of Christians and Jews and the Interfaith Network for the UK, who **work together** to open discussions and heal divisions between faiths.
- By sharing basic understandings that God created all humans **equal**.
- Celebration of festivals and worship where different faiths take part in services which show **respect** and **unity** for each other.
- Muslim Council of Britain encourages Muslims to take an active role in UK society and not be isolated as a faith group.
- Encouraging **representation** of different faith groups in jobs such as the police to allow good role models and unity.

An example of religious community cohesion

Bolton Christian Community Cohesion Project

Education and youth: Provide a free family fun day for diverse communities.

Leisure: A 'night cafe' project that provides a safe place for people to go and addresses issues of anti social behaviour.

Workplace: Supports hospitals, the university and town centres from the Bolton community.

Now try this

1 'Religious people should work harder to promote community cohesion'. In your answer you should refer to at least one religion.

(i) Do you agree? Give reasons for your opinion. **(d, 3 marks)**

(ii) Give reasons why some people may disagree with you. **(3 marks)**

2 Do you think religions can work together to help community cohesion? Give two reasons for your point of view. **(b, 4 marks)**

Try and give examples to help develop your answers. You could use specific examples of successful attempts at community cohesion to support your answer.

Religion and community cohesion in the media

Many television and radio programmes deal with religious and community cohesion issues. But do these programmes treat religion **fairly**?

How media programmes present religious and community cohesion issues

NEWS PROGRAMMES	present issues of public concern but should not encourage racism or ill feeling, e.g. reporting on riots.
DISCUSSION PROGRAMMES	many TV debates have religious themes, e.g. about blasphemy.
SOAP OPERAS	are often used to promote understanding or to air an issue that is highlighted in society, e.g. religious attitudes to women.
TELEVISION DOCUMENTARIES	programmes such as Everyman, Witness and Panorama deal with controversial issues.
RADIO	programmes on stations such as Radio 4 or one-off programmes deal with religious and community themes, e.g. inter faith marriage.

Remember – you have studied how the media dealt with one issue arising from community cohesion. Make sure you also revise this!

What issues may be shown in the media?

- Racial prejudice and tension.
- Religious tolerance.
- Religious families coming to terms with being in a community without compromising their beliefs.
- Religious and community themes.
- Domestic violence or attitudes towards women.

Biased?

Sometimes media programmes are accused of only showing **one side** of an argument or a biased presentation of an issue. This gives a distorted view of what is really happening.

Issues need to be dealt with sensitively and accurately to ensure that ideas such as racism or hatred of other religions are not promoted.

Weekly Moan

Mixed marriages cause global vampire outbreak!

Now try this

1 Do you think the media is biased against religion? Give two reasons for your point of view. **(b, 4 marks)**

2 Explain, using examples, how the media presents an issue of religion and community cohesion. **(c, 8 marks)**

Think carefully about how the media presents religious issues – is it mainly in a positive or negative way?

Had a look ☐ Nearly there ☐ Nailed it! ☐

Key words

It is important that you learn the key words for each topic. This is so you can explain what they mean for (a) type questions and use the key words in your answers to other questions to explain ideas fully.

Key words	Definitions
community cohesion	a common vision and shared sense of belonging for all groups in society
discrimination	treating people less favourably because of their ethnicity/gender/colour/sexuality/age/class
ethnic minority	a member of an ethnic group (race) which is much smaller than the majority group
interfaith marriages	a marriage in which the husband and wife are from different religions
multi-ethnic society	many different races and cultures living together in one society
multi-faith society	many different religions living together in one society
prejudice	believing some people are inferior or superior without even knowing them
racial harmony	different races/colours living together happily
racism	the belief that some races are superior to others
religious freedom	the right to practise your religion and change your religion
religious pluralism	accepting all religions as having an equal right to coexist
sexism	discriminating against people because of their gender (being male or female)

Exam skills: (a) questions and SPaG

Your exam paper is divided into four sections. Each section contains two full questions and you must choose one of these to answer in each section. You need to spend about 20 minutes answering each question. Each question has 4 parts, (a), (b), (c) and (d).

Spelling, punctuation and grammar

Before we look at (a) questions you need to know about some extra marks you can earn. In Section 1 of the Unit 1 exam paper, there are 4 marks available for spelling, punctuation and grammar. To be successful here, your spelling, punctuation and grammar need to be really good. Make sure that you use formal written English and not slang or text-speak, for example. You need to use these to help make what you want to say very clear. Also try to use a good range of key words accurately.

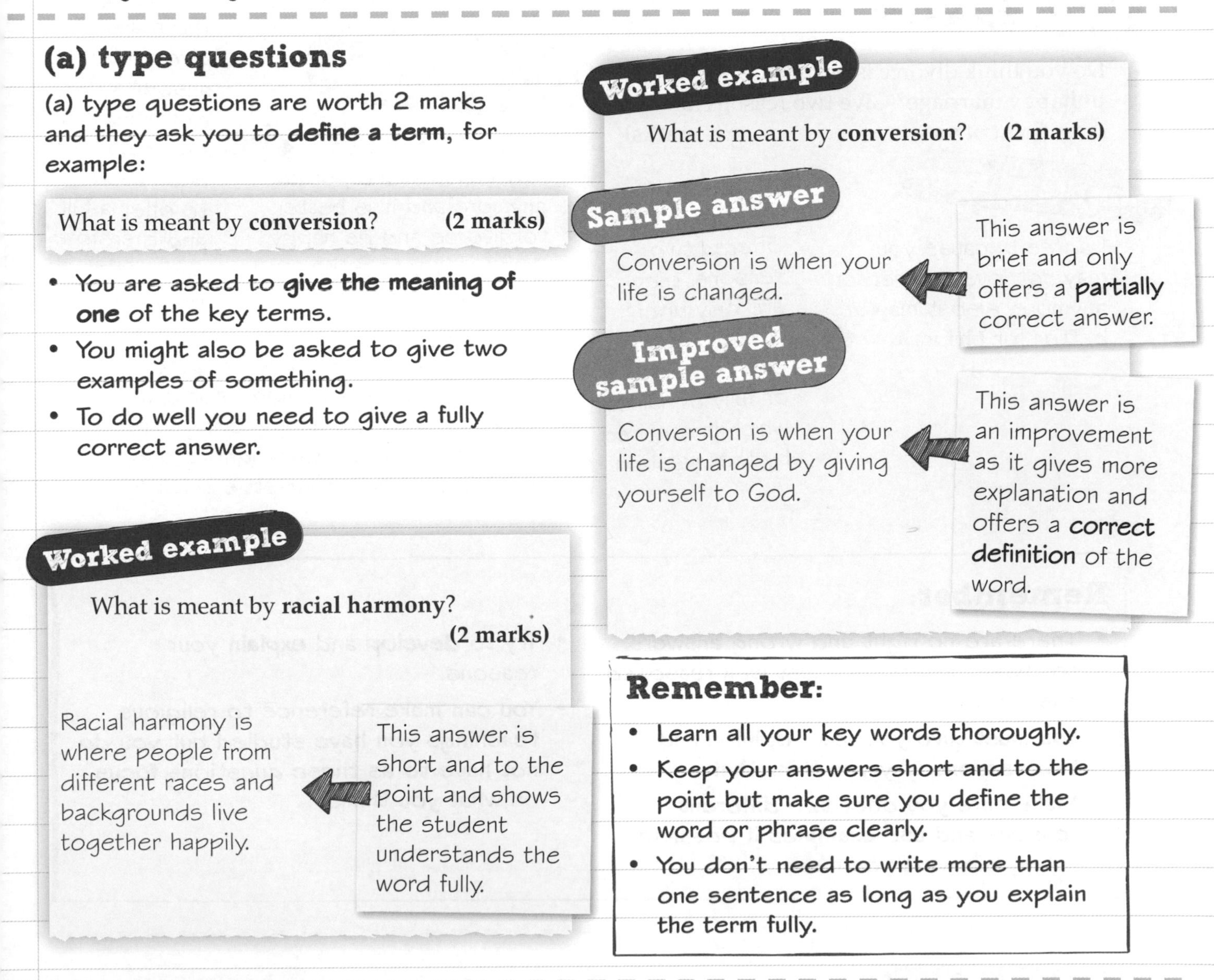

(a) type questions

(a) type questions are worth 2 marks and they ask you to **define a term**, for example:

What is meant by **conversion**? **(2 marks)**

- You are asked to **give the meaning of one** of the key terms.
- You might also be asked to give two examples of something.
- To do well you need to give a fully correct answer.

Worked example

What is meant by **racial harmony**? **(2 marks)**

Racial harmony is where people from different races and backgrounds live together happily.

This answer is short and to the point and shows the student understands the word fully.

Worked example

What is meant by **conversion**? **(2 marks)**

Sample answer

Conversion is when your life is changed.

This answer is brief and only offers a **partially** correct answer.

Improved sample answer

Conversion is when your life is changed by giving yourself to God.

This answer is an improvement as it gives more explanation and offers a **correct definition** of the word.

Remember:

- Learn all your key words thoroughly.
- Keep your answers short and to the point but make sure you define the word or phrase clearly.
- You don't need to write more than one sentence as long as you explain the term fully.

Now try this

1 You could make yourself a set of flash cards with the word on one side and the definition on the other to help you learn the key terms.

Exam skills: (b) questions

(b) type questions are worth 4 marks and ask for **your opinion** on a point of view.

Applying your skills

To do well on a 4-mark question, you should:

- Give **your own** opinion.
- Give **two reasons** to support your opinion.
- Try not to give brief reasons. Instead aim to offer **well-developed** reasons. Try to explain fully the reason you are giving.
- You can also give an example to support your reason, as a way of developing your answer.

Worked example

Do you think divorce is better than an unhappy marriage? Give **two** reasons for your point of view. **(4 marks)**

Sample answer

I agree because you may not love the person anymore. Also it may be better for children.

Although the student has offered two reasons, they are only brief reasons. Neither one is developed or fully explained, which is required by the question.

Improved sample answer

I agree because you may not love the person anymore and it is better to divorce and be happy than to stay together and keep suffering.

Also it may be better for children if parents divorce because it may make their upbringing more stable. It is better to have two happy loving parents than two who are always fighting and arguing, which might unsettle children.

The reasons given in this answer are explained, and examples have been used to offer a full and therefore successful response.

Remember:

- There are no right and wrong answers to these questions – just well reasoned answers.
- You **must** give your own **opinion** and **two reasons** why you think that.
- Make sure you offer two **different** reasons and use **examples** if possible to explain what you mean.
- Try to **develop** and **explain** your reasons.
- You can make reference to religious teachings you have studied but you do not have to as these questions focus on what **you** think.

Now try this

1 Do you think men and women are treated equally in society today? Give two reasons for your opinion. **(4 marks)**

Try to apply the hints above to this question, building up your answer to achieve full marks.

Exam skills: (c) questions

(c) questions are worth 8 marks. They ask you to **explain** a particular belief or idea.

Applying your skills

To do well on an 8-mark or (c) type question you must try to:

- **Explain** ideas fully – don't just make a list: explain how and why, use phrases such as 'this is because'.
- Give **up to four** reasons to support your opinion.
- The **fewer reasons** you give the **more well-developed** your answers need to be.
- Use relevant **examples** to support your points. This will help develop your answer.
- Start a **new paragraph** for each point. This makes it easier to check your answer at the end.
- Make sure you **read** the question carefully!

QWC

In the (c) questions you will also be assessed on your Quality of Written Communication (QWC). (You'll see a * next to the question.) You need to:

- Express your understanding clearly and using a good standard of English.
- Check your handwriting, spelling, punctuation and grammar.
- Use specialist vocabulary and religious key terms.
- Plan and structure your answer carefully to suit the question.

Remember:

- Include a **variety** of reasons.
- Try not to just give brief reasons.
- Learn the content thoroughly.
- Learn some key quotes from the Bible or Qur'an to support what you say.
- There are marks available for QWCs.

Worked example

Explain why Christians believe they should promote racial harmony.

Christians are against racism, where people are treated differently. The Bible teaches that God created everyone. So, everyone should be treated equally, regardless of their race.

Jesus treated everyone he met equally and with love. The parable of the Good Samaritan teaches Christians to treat all people the same regardless of race.

Jesus treated everybody equally and with respect. For example, he talked with people like the tax collectors who were hated by society. Christians believe that everyone is a brother in the Church so they should work to promote racial harmony to make everyone feel as if they belong.

Here each point has its own paragraph. The students' reasons are well-explained and supported with examples.

The answer is clear and this is shown through the structured answer and use of key words.

Now try this

1 Explain how Christians respond to the problem of evil and suffering. **(8 marks)**

Exam skills: (d) questions

(d) type questions are worth 6 marks. They ask for **your opinion** and for you to also consider an **alternative** point of view.

Applying your skills

To do well on a 6-mark (d) question:

- Spend **equal time** on answering part (i) as you do part (ii).
- Offer **your opinion** and views on the statement.
- Show that you know why some people hold **different views** to you and why.
- **Refer to a religion** – you need to include at least one religious view.
- Give **evidence** or **examples** to support both your view and alternative opinions.

For each part of your answer:

A partial answer = 1 simple reason.

An improved answer = 2 simple reasons or 1 developed reason.

An even better answer = 3 simple reasons or 1 developed and 1 simple reason.

Worked example

'Religious parents should make sure their children are brought up to believe in God'.
In your answer you should refer to at least one religion.

i. Do you agree? Give reasons for your opinion. **(3 marks)**

I agree because Muslims believe they will be judged on how they bring up their children so it is important to do this the way Allah wants. Secondly, it will ensure that faith is passed to the next generation and be strengthened. Finally, Islamic parents want to be sure that their children will go to them in Heaven so try to bring them up within the faith.

ii. Give reasons why some people may disagree with you. **(3 marks)**

However, other people may disagree because they might feel that religion should not be forced onto children and they should be allowed to choose when they are older. Also they may grow up to rebel against their parents in the future if religion has been forced on them and so they may turn away from religion.

Remember:

- Try to give up to **three** reasons.
- Have at least one **religious** view.
- Clearly **separate** the two parts of your answer.
- Give **reasons** to support your opinion. However, the **fewer** reasons you give the **more** well-developed your answers need to be.
- Think about the reasons you have learned about in class.

This first part of the answer offers at least three reasons for their view, some of which are developed.

The second part of the answer offers two distinct developed ideas to show why some people may disagree with the statement.

Now try this

1 'It is not possible for so many different faiths to live peacefully in the UK today.'
In your answer you should refer to at least one religion

(i) Do you agree? Give reasons for your opinion **(3 marks)**

(ii) Give reasons why some people may disagree with you. **(3 marks)**

Christians and the Bible

The Christian holy book, the Bible, carries **authority** for Christians as it was written by God and some use it to make moral decisions (what is right and wrong).

Using the Bible to make moral decisions:

1. Many Christians believe the Bible is the **word of God**. It contains teachings on how to live. For example:
   - *The New Testament offers moral guidance and teachings on how Christians should behave (e.g. St Peter and St Paul).*
2. The Bible has **authority** from God about what Christians should believe and how they should live. For example:
   - *It contains laws that tell Christians how they should act (e.g. the Ten Commandments). Jesus' teachings and examples are shown which Christians should follow.*
3. **Some** Christians believe that **only** the Bible should be used to decide what is right, wrong and what they should believe.
   - *The Bible comes from God so it is the only thing that can be trusted.*
   - *The Bible has been handed down for hundreds of years and has kept Christians on the right path.*
   - *God's truth does not change.*

The Decalogue

1	2
You shall have no other Gods before me.	You shall not worship idols
3	**4**
You shall not misuse the name of the Lord	Remember the Sabbath day and keep it holy
5	**6**
Honour your father and mother	You shall not murder
7	**8**
You shall not commit adultery	You shall not steal
9	**10**
You shall not bear false witness (lie)	You shall not covet (be envious)

Christians will look to the Ten Commandments (the Decalogue) in the Bible to help them make decisions.

The Bible's authority

Christians have **different** opinions on the authority of the Bible:

The Bible is literally the word of God and is totally right. Some Christians believe God directly told the authors what to write.

The Bible is the word of God but needs to be interpreted by the Church.

The Bible was inspired by God and gives guidance about how to live but needs to be adapted for modern life.

Now try this

1 What is the **Bible**? **(a, 2 marks)**

2 Explain why Christians believe they should use the Bible when making moral decisions. **(c, 8 marks)**

Remember, there are extra marks available for Section 1 of your exam paper for spelling, punctuation and grammar. Make sure you leave time to check these in your answers, and that you use key words where possible.

Christians and the authority of the Church

All Christians believe the Bible has authority in their lives but also look to the Church for help and advice when making moral decisions. Some think the Church is the **only** true authority.

How the Church guides Christians

1. Talking to other Christians.
2. Listening to the priest or vicar.
3. Praying and worshipping together.
4. Accepting the authority of the Church to explain and teach God's word.

How different Churches decide on moral issues

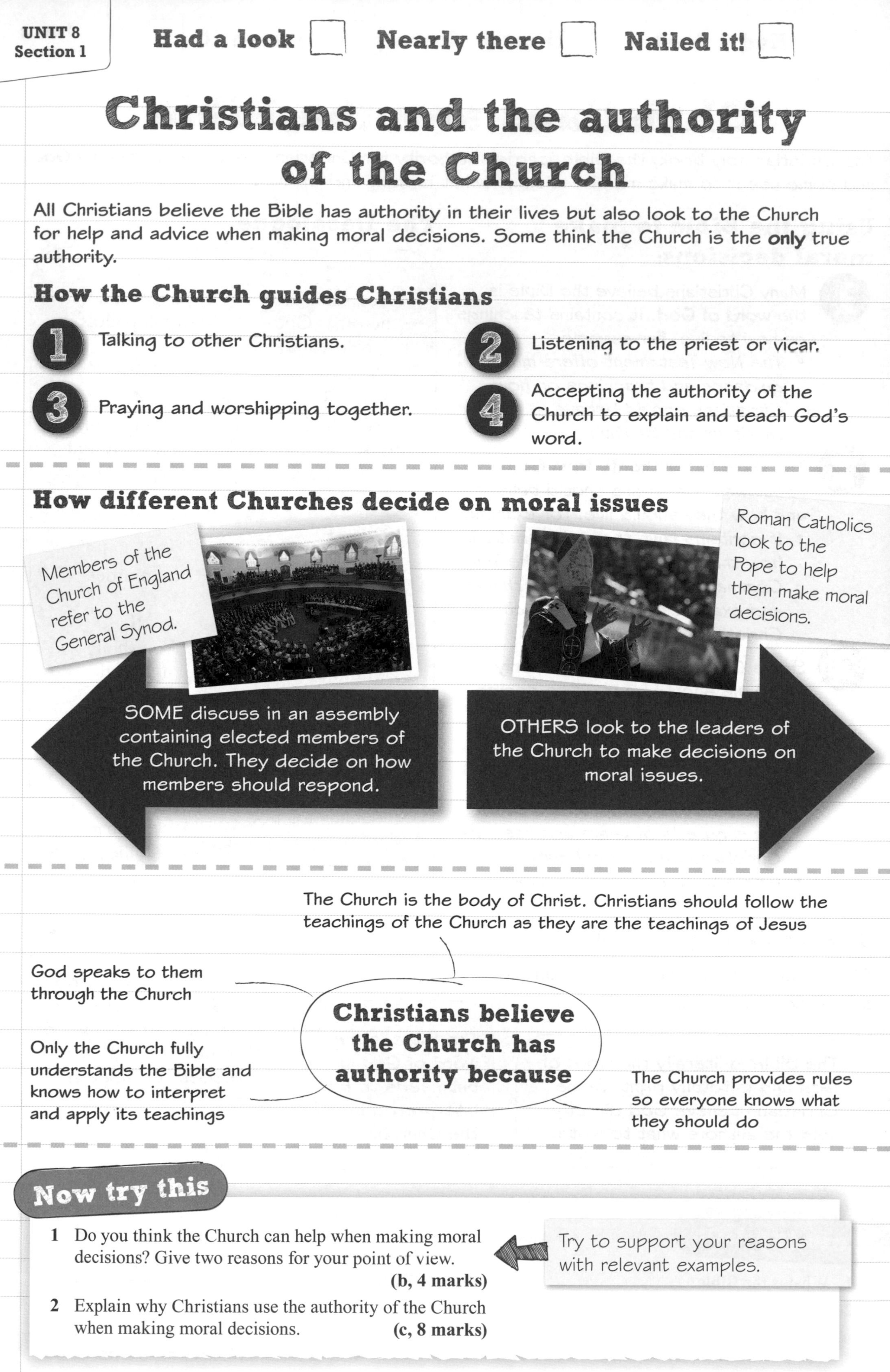

Members of the Church of England refer to the General Synod.

SOME discuss in an assembly containing elected members of the Church. They decide on how members should respond.

Roman Catholics look to the Pope to help them make moral decisions.

OTHERS look to the leaders of the Church to make decisions on moral issues.

Christians believe the Church has authority because

- The Church is the body of Christ. Christians should follow the teachings of the Church as they are the teachings of Jesus
- God speaks to them through the Church
- Only the Church fully understands the Bible and knows how to interpret and apply its teachings
- The Church provides rules so everyone knows what they should do

Now try this

1. Do you think the Church can help when making moral decisions? Give two reasons for your point of view. **(b, 4 marks)**
2. Explain why Christians use the authority of the Church when making moral decisions. **(c, 8 marks)**

Try to support your reasons with relevant examples.

Christians and conscience

Some Christians believe that their conscience is given to them by God. They believe this is the **most** important guide to making moral decisions.

What is the conscience?

- The inner feeling or sense of what is right or wrong.
- Christians believe it is the voice of God within us.
- It is the way both religious and non-religious people can judge their moral actions.
- It makes us feel guilty if we do things that are wrong.
- Some Christians believe that conscience is the most important guide when making moral decisions.

The conscience is an individual guide to whether an action is right or wrong.

How Christians use conscience to make moral decisions

Christians believe they should consult the Bible, look at the teachings of the Church but in the end follow their conscience.

The Bible + The Church + Conscience

Conscientious objectors

Conscientious objectors are an example of when some Christians use conscience as their main guide when making moral decisions.

These are people who object to fighting and refuse to fight in a war because they think it is against God's moral code and their conscience tells them this is the correct action.

Kevin Benderman, a former US soldier, received a prison sentence for refusing to deploy to Iraq in 2005.

Now try this

1 What is meant by **conscience**? **(a, 2 marks)**

2 'Conscience is not always reliable when making moral decisions' In your answer, you should refer to at least one religion.

(i) Do you agree? Give two reasons for your opinion. **(d, 3 marks)**

(ii) Give reasons why some people might disagree with you. **(3 marks)**

When answering this question, consider the pros and cons of using the conscience as a source of authority. Why might other sources perhaps be more reliable and more accurate for religious believers to use?

Christians and Situation Ethics

Situation Ethics is a Christian approach to making moral decisions. It was put forward by American Christian minister Joseph Fletcher during the 1960s, a time of great social change. Some Christians decide to only use this principle when making moral decisions.

- Love should be the only consideration when making moral decisions.
- A good action is one which aims to do the most loving thing.
- A person should only obey the rules of the Bible or teaching of the Church if it results in the most loving action.

Many Christians would use Situation Ethics alongside other ways of making moral decisions. Some, however, use **only** Situation Ethics

It is similar to the 'Golden Rule' taught by Jesus which says '...do unto others what you would have them do to you...' (Matthew 7:12)

Jesus seemed to follow Situation Ethics, for example when he ignored the teachings of the Bible and acted in a most loving way in the case where a woman was being accused of adultery (John 8:1–11)

Reasons FOR using Situation Ethics

✔ Every situation is judged individually.

✔ As **love** is the main principle, it follows a genuine Christian action.

✔ Love is an easy principle to apply and remember in all situations.

✔ Doing the most loving thing will appeal to people as a positive idea.

Reasons AGAINST using Situation Ethics

✘ It is impossible to predict what will happen in every example, which is what this requires.

✘ In theory, anything a person felt was the 'most loving thing' could be justified including adultery or murder.

✘ It is not so easy to apply Situation Ethics in everyday cases where we are used to having rules.

Now try this

1 What is meant by **social change**? **(a, 2 marks)**

2 Explain why some Christians use only Situation Ethics when making moral decisions. **(c, 8 marks)**

Christians and the variety of moral authorities

Moral dilemmas are rarely simple so many Christians consult **all** authorities available to them.

The four types of moral authorities

1. Law and teaching of the Bible.
2. Teachings and guidance of the Church.
3. The conscience.
4. Principles of Situation Ethics.

Why use a variety of moral authorities?

- Christians believe they must live life according to God.
- Different Christians believe different sources of authority contain advice and help on what God wants.
- They may use **one** source of authority or refer to a **combination**.

- **Some** Christians believe the Bible is literally **true**. They think it contains complete guidance from God. They are likely to use this as their **main** source of authority on how to live and make moral decisions.
- **Other** Christians may believe the Bible contains important truths but feel it **shouldn't** be followed exactly as written and may use the guidance of **other** authorities when making moral decisions.

The different authorities provide guidance on how Christians should live.

Good deeds

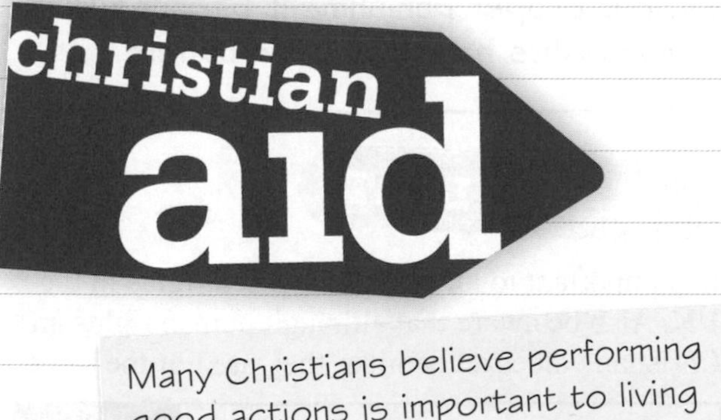

Many Christians believe performing good actions is important to living a moral life. They help others, doing voluntary work and campaigning.

Spiritual development

Other Christians believe moral development is about spiritual rather than social issues. They will concentrate on building a closer relationship with God by praying and worshipping regularly.

Now try this

1 Do you think it is better to use a variety of methods to make a moral decision?
Give two reasons for your opinion. **(b, 4 marks)**

To be successful on a (b) question, try to give **two** reasons for your opinion, with examples. Think about the different ways in which Christians make moral decisions and why.

Had a look Nearly there  Nailed it!

Human rights in the UK

Human rights are the basic rights and freedoms to which all human beings are entitled.

The United Nations

The United Nations Declaration of Human Rights says that all humans are born **free** and **equal** in dignity and rights.

All citizens of the UK are entitled to:

- life
- food
- liberty / free speech
- racial / sexual / religious equality
- education
- health care
- privacy

The Human Rights Act

In the UK today, human rights are protected by law. Most are covered by the Human Rights Act 1998. Anyone who feels their rights have been infringed or abused can appeal to the European Court of Human Rights.

The Human Rights Act in practice

The law on human rights has had a positive effect on issues of child prostitution and illegal immigration.

However, there has been controversy about issues where human rights need to be overruled when national security is at risk, such as in cases of terrorism.

Some people believe that suspected terrorists may not be entitled to human rights. Others say that anti-terrorism acts abuse human rights.

Criticisms

The Human Rights Act has been criticised because some might argue that it has allowed criminals to get away without proper punishment because their human rights have not been upheld.

EXAM ALERT!

It is important to know about human rights in the **UK**. Also be aware that although human rights and Christian values are similar, they are **not** the same.

Students have struggled with this topic in recent exams – **be prepared!** ResultsPlus

Now try this

1 What are **human rights**? **(a, 2 marks)**

2 Do you think everyone in society should be entitled to the same human rights? Give **two** reasons for your opinion. **(b, 4 marks)**

Why human rights are important to Christians

Human rights are important to Christians and many Christian principles are mirrored within human rights.

Human rights are important to Christians because:

1. They believe every human being is created by God in his image and deserves respect.
2. They believe God loves everyone equally so all should be treated equally.

3. The teachings of the Bible, for example the Ten Commandments (The Decalogue) support most human rights laws.

The Bible and human rights

- The Parable of the Sheep and Goats teaches that it is the moral **duty** of Christians to help people in need. (Matthew 25:40)
- Jesus taught the Golden Rule showing all humans are worthy of value and **respect** and human rights are important.

...do unto others what you would have done unto you...

Matthew 7:12

However the UK is a multi-faith and multi-ethnic society, which is run in a **secular** and not religious way. So, some Christians believe that Christian values should **not** be imposed on the government.

Christians who have worked to improve human rights

Many Christians have worked to establish what we now know as human rights.

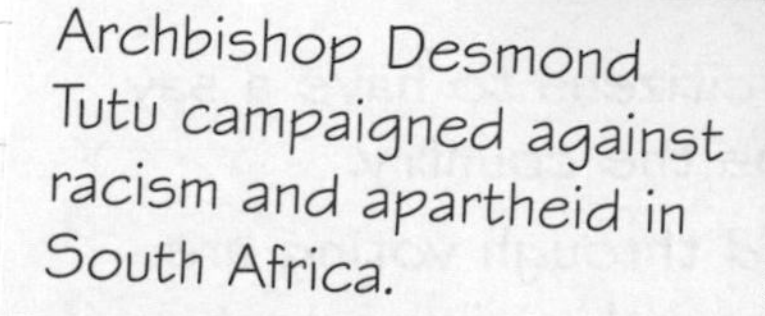

Archbishop Desmond Tutu campaigned against racism and apartheid in South Africa.

Now try this

1 Explain why human rights are important to Christians. **(c, 8 marks)**

2 'Human rights laws should also be in agreement with religious teachings.' In your answer you should refer to at least one religion.

(i) Do you agree? Give reasons for your opinion. **(d, 3 marks)**

(ii) Give reasons why some people may disagree with you. **(3 marks)**

Try to write a new paragraph for each point you make. This makes it easier to go back and check that you've said what you wanted to say and that your answer makes sense.

Had a look ☐ Nearly there ☐ Nailed it! ☐

The importance of democratic and electoral processes

Democracy is the political system used in the UK. It is important to take part in democratic and electoral processes because these give all citizens a say in who runs the country.

Democracy in the UK

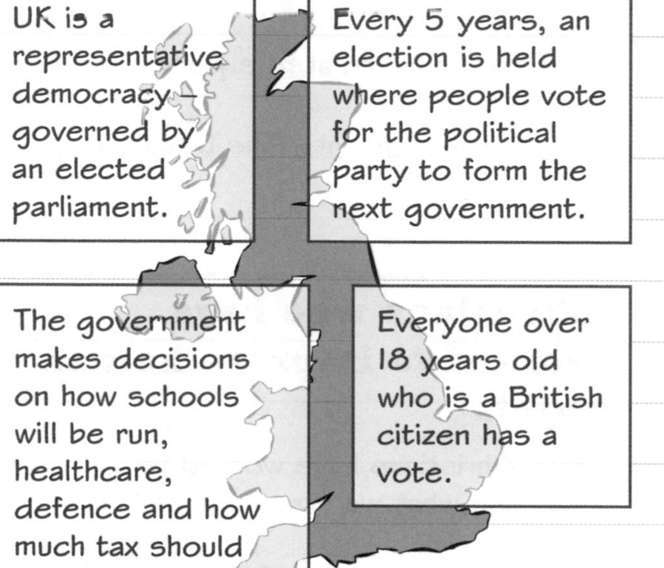

There are three main political parties. Each party puts forward its own views.

Some views of the main political parties.

Labour Party
The state should help the poor and provide hospitals and school for all.

Conservative Party
The state should encourage people to look after themselves and only provide what people cannot pay for themselves.

Liberal Democrat Party
Green issues are important and the government and individuals need to work together to help everyone.

Why it is important to take part

- Voting allows citizens to have a say about who runs the country.
- People elected through voting are responsible for making important decisions that affect everyone.
- Issues include taxes, benefits, rubbish collection, health treatment, schools and the armed forces.
- **Change** can only be brought about through the democratic process.

How else can people take part?

- Write to or meet MPs to discuss issues of concern.
- Lobby – which means to influence government decisions. This could be writing letters or taking part in public demonstrations/petitions.
- Become members of political parties which support their views.
- Stand for election themselves.

Now try this

1 What is meant by **electoral processes**? **(a, 2 marks)**

2 Do you think people younger than 18 should be allowed to vote? Give two reasons for your point of view. **(b, 4 marks)**

This is a controversial question. Think about what benefit those who are under 18 could bring to an election. Try to support your **two** reasons with examples.

Christian teachings on moral duties and responsibilities

Christians believe that God gives them moral duties and responsibilities which they must carry out. Christianity stresses the importance of **faith** and **good works**.

The Golden Rule

The Golden Rule

The Golden Rule states '…do to others what you would have them do to you…' meaning that Christians should treat others as they would wish to be treated. (Matthew 7:12)

2 The Parable of the Sheep and the Goats

Jesus taught through this story that God will at the end separate his people into those who have **helped others** (the sheep) and those who have not (the goats). Christians have a duty to help those in need when they can. (Matthew 25:31–46)

Christian teachings on moral duties and responsibilities

3 Am I my brother's keeper?: St Paul

St Paul taught that Christians should not stand by and do nothing while others suffer. He used the example of Cain and Abel to warn Christians that they have a moral duty to actively **care** for others. Cain killed his brother Abel then denied he had anything to do with it, saying it was not up to him to care for others.

THE TEN COMMANDMENTS

The Ten Commandments also stress the importance of moral duties. They include teachings such as 'honour your parents', 'do not murder' and 'do not steal'. Christians are expected to follow these in their everyday lives. (Exodus 20:2–17).

Now try this

1 Do you think 'the Golden Rule' is still relevant today? Give two reasons for your point of view. **(b, 4 marks)**

Make sure you offer **your opinion** and explain reasons why you hold your view. You could begin by giving a statement that shows this is your opinion, and then give **examples** to support your two reasons.

The nature of genetic engineering

Genetic engineering is a very **controversial** issue because although it seems to offer great potential, many people have concerns about it.

What is genetic engineering?

- It is the process where the structure and characteristics of genes are changed.
- Genes can be added, replaced or taken away. Genes that cause disorders can be removed or improvements made.
- The UK government has strict guidelines on genetically modified (GM) crops.

Cloning

- A clone is an exact copy of something.
- Reproductive cloning is a technology used to create an animal or plant with an identical genetic makeup to another.
- Therapeutic cloning is the cloning of embryos to harvest stem cells. Stem cells develop in an embryo.

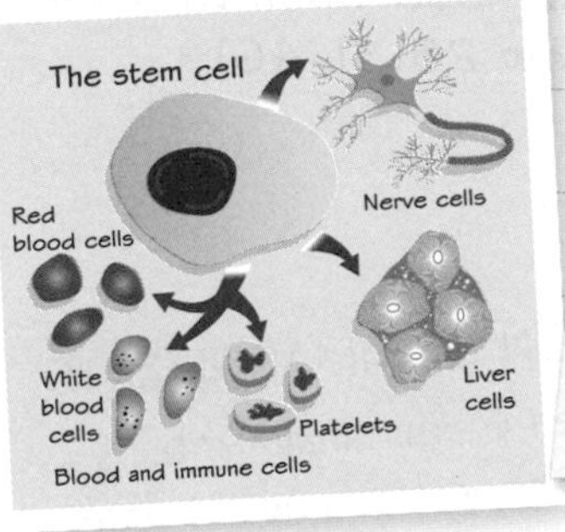

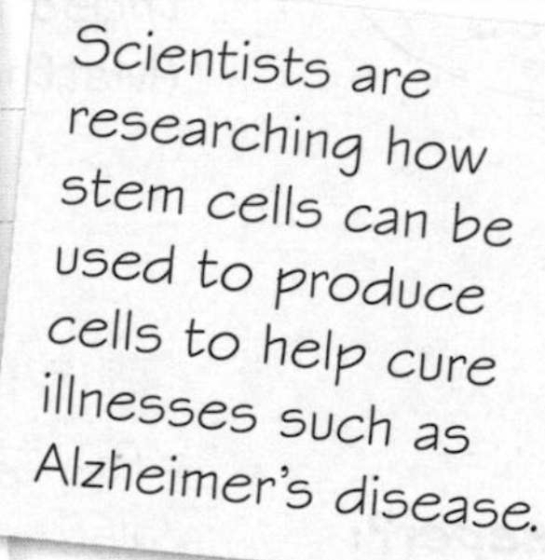

What could we do with it?

- Genetic disorders may be cured using gene therapy to replace missing genes.
- Hormones and proteins can be produced, for example insulin for diabetics.
- Genes can be inserted to grow human parts on animals for organ transplants.
- Inherited disorders like cystic fibrosis could be removed from embryos.
- It could be used to grow crops that are resistant to pests and disease, or that grow in harsh climates or on infertile land.

Concerns

- Nature is complex and we do not know the exact long-term effects of genetic engineering and cloning.
- These technologies could be dangerous in the wrong hands because they could be used to produce biological weapons.
- Who makes decisions over what is defective and what is not? There is currently no guidance.
- This could lead to 'designer babies' with people wanting certain characteristics for their children.

Now try this

1. What is **genetic engineering**? **(a, 2 marks)**
2. Do you agree with genetic engineering? Give two reasons for your point of view. **(b, 4 marks)**

To be successful on (a) questions, make sure you learn your key words thoroughly.

Christian attitudes to genetic engineering

Genetic engineering is a controversial topic for Christians. Views are divided about whether it should happen or not.

Christian beliefs

All Christians believe life is **sacred** and therefore should be **respected**. Some Christians may accept genetic engineering in certain circumstances, while others may oppose it entirely.

Even those who support genetic engineering believe it should only be done for reasons such as healing the sick or feeding the hungry.

Different Christian viewpoints on genetic engineering and cloning

FOR

- God gave humans dominion (power) over the world. Christians believe that as long as it does not cause harm, some forms of genetic engineering, such as GM crops, would be acceptable.
- The Golden Rule is '...do to others what you would have them do to you...' For some Christians this could mean genetic engineering to cure diseases and disorders is acceptable.
- Jesus healed people and Christians believe they should follow his example by trying to improve the health of others.
- Some Christians believe that God has given us the gift of knowledge and we should use this and technology to help develop and possibly save human life.

AGAINST

- Only God can create life and humans should not 'play God'.
- Life is sacred and special and created by God so humans should not be doing anything against this.
- Some Christians, such as Catholics, believe life begins at conception and are opposed to anything that involves research on embryos when some are then discarded.
- Most Christians would be against genetic engineering curing 'defects' that don't cause suffering, such as being short sighted.

Now try this

1 'Christians should never agree with genetic engineering'. In your answer you should refer to at least one religion.

(i) Do you agree? Give reasons for your opinion. **(d, 3 marks)**

(ii) Give reasons why some people may disagree with you. **(3 marks)**

Genetic engineering is a complex issue which Christians are often divided on. Try to show this in your answer. Make sure you clearly separate your own opinion and why others may disagree. Try to give examples to support your reasons.

Had a look ☐ Nearly there ☐ Nailed it! ☐

Key words

It is important that you learn the key words for each topic. This is so you can explain what they mean for (a) type questions and use the key words in your answers to other questions to explain ideas fully.

Key words	Definitions
Bible	the holy book of Christians
Church	the community of Christians (church with a small 'c' means a Christian place of worship)
conscience	an inner feeling of the rightness or wrongness of an action
the Decalogue	the Ten Commandments
democratic processes	the ways in which all citizens can take part in government (usually through elections)
electoral processes	the ways in which voting is organised
the Golden Rule	the teaching of Jesus that you should treat others as you would like them to treat you
human rights	the rights and freedoms to which everyone is entitled
political party	a group which tries to be elected into power on the basis of its policies (e.g. Labour, Conservative)
pressure group	a group formed to influence government policy on a particular issue
Situation Ethics	the idea that Christians should base moral decisions on what is the most loving thing to do
social change	the way in which society has changed and is changing (and also the possibilities for future change)

Global warming

Global warming, also known as climate change, is the increase in temperature of the Earth's atmosphere.

Causes

- Many scientists believe that the burning of fossil fuels by humans increases greenhouse gases, such as carbon dioxide, in the atmosphere.
- Some scientists believe that the rise in temperature is natural and the climate has always been in a state of change.

Effects

1. In polar regions the **ice melts** and increases the sea level which means that some land may be submerged.

2. Some hotter areas suffering **drought** and others suffering excessive **rain** and **flooding**. This could result in shortages of food and then famine.

3. Increase in **extreme weather** events such as hurricanes and flash floods.

4. Some animals and plants may **die out** if they can't adapt.

Solutions

We need to reduce the amount of energy being used and increase the use of 'clean' fuels.

1. **Individually** – turn off electrical appliances when not in use, walk rather than use vehicles, support environmental charities, lobby the government for change.
2. **Government and organisations** – set laws for factories to reduce energy, work together to try and reduce energy usage.
3. **Scientists** – research into the causes and consequences of climate change so we understand more about it and can do more to prevent it.

Now try this

1 What is **global warming**? **(a, 2 marks)**

2 Do you think global warming is a big problem? Give two reasons for your point of view. **(b, 4 marks)**

It is worth beginning your answer with a statement to show that this is your own opinion, for example 'I think global warming is a big problem because…'.

Pollution

Pollution is the contamination of the environment which damages and spoils the world. The majority of pollution is caused by waste – products humans do not want.

Forms of pollution

Waste

Increase in waste that is not biodegradable or recyclable. Waste takes up space, spreads disease and releases dangerous chemicals. Examples: new technology products like computers.

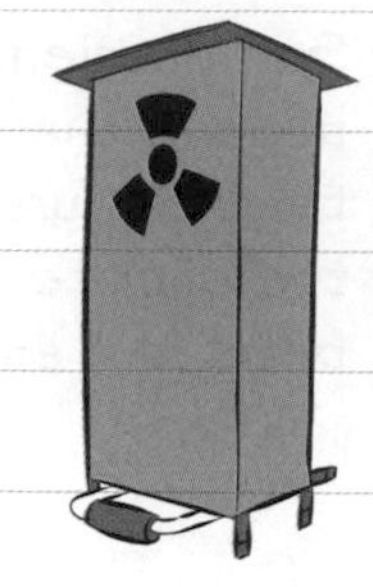

Land

Land or soil pollution leads to poor plant growth and threatens animal habitats. Examples: littering, pesticides and radioactive waste.

Air

Substances or chemicals released into the atmosphere threaten the chemical balance of the air. Leads to: acid rain caused by burning fossil fuels; and smog, which affects humans and animals. Examples: vehicle fumes, CFCs, burning fossil fuels and waste from power stations.

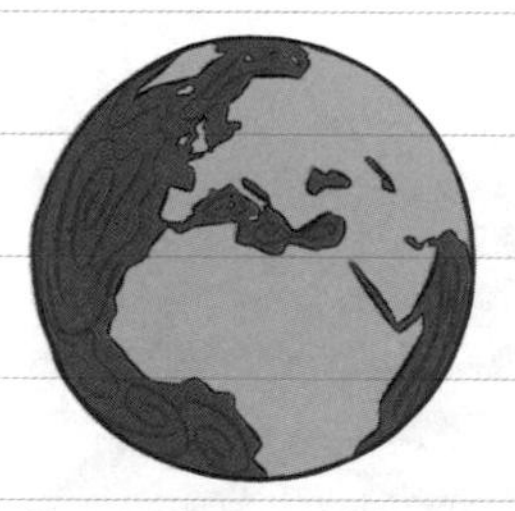

Water

Contaminated rivers, lakes, oceans and reservoirs. This affects the water quality and the plants and animals that live there. Examples: chemicals, fertilisers, oil, sewage and eutrophication (too many nutrients affect the environment: algae grow and the bacteria that break nutrients down use up the oxygen that fish need).

Solutions

Create less waste

Recycle as much as possible. Reduce packaging. Re-use as much as possible.

Government action

Anti-pollution laws to limit the amount of pollution, and severe penalties if these laws are broken.

Alternative energy sources

Use of renewable, clean sources such as solar and wind power to reduce waste and pollution.

Alternative manufacturing methods

Research into ways of manufacturing that cause less waste or that remove waste more efficiently.

Now try this

1. Do you think we should do more to help the environment? Give two reasons for your point of view. **(b, 4 marks)**
2. Explain how humans contribute to pollution. **(c, 8 marks)**

Make sure you give **two** reasons for your point of view and perhaps give an example to support each one.

Natural resources

Natural resources are naturally occurring materials such as oil and fertile land, which can be used to produce energy. There are two types: renewable and non-renewable.

Renewable resources

These can replace themselves or be replaced by humans.

- wind power
- solar power (from the Sun)
- wave power
- water power
- fertile land
- wood.

✔ Advantages

They will never run out and most provide '**clean**' energy, which doesn't cause pollution.

✘ Disadvantages

Many are only effective in certain areas (e.g. where it's windy or sunny). They can also be more **expensive**.

Non-renewable resources

These **cannot** be replaced once used.

- coal
- oil
- gas
- elements, minerals and rocks (such as uranium for nuclear power).

✔ Advantages

Some (e.g. metals) can be recycled and they are useful to humans for transport, electricity, buildings and everyday products.

✘ Disadvantages

They are **scarce**. Once they are used up, they cannot be replaced and will be gone forever. Many cause pollution.

Issues

1. Humans are very reliant on non-renewable energy sources.
2. If they are used at their current rate, they will run out.
3. This will have an enormous impact and effect on the planet and human life.

Possible solutions: conservation

Conservation involves protecting and preserving **natural resources** and the environment for future generations. →

- Use renewable energy sources.
- Conserve electricity.
- Walk or cycle rather than drive.
- Use products made from renewable sources.

Now try this

1 What are **natural resources**? **(a, 2 marks)**

2 'We should stop using non-renewable resources now to save them for future generations'. In your answer you should refer to at least one religion.

(i) Do you agree? Give reasons for your opinion. **(d, 3 marks)**

(ii) Give reasons why some people may disagree with you. **(3 marks)**

Make sure you offer your own opinion to answer this question, and develop your reasons. Do the same for part (ii) and show why some people may hold a different view to you.

Had a look ☐ Nearly there ☐ Nailed it! ☐

Christian teachings on stewardship and attitudes to the environment

Christians believe in 'creation' – the idea that the Earth and everything in it was created by God –and therefore they should look after the Earth.

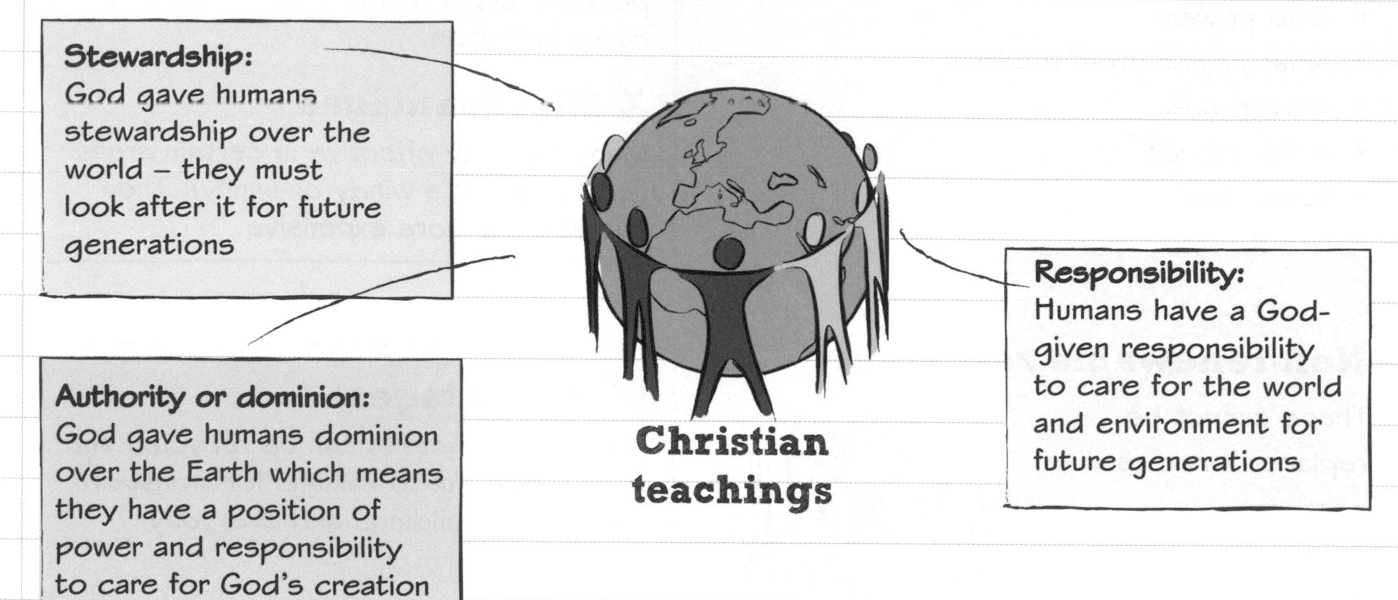

The effect on Christian attitudes to the environment

The Bible teaches Christians that they should:

- Take care of the environment because it is a gift from God.
- Share the resources of the world more equally because Jesus taught Christians to love and help each other.
- Conserve the Earth's natural resources for future generations.
- Reduce pollution to help the environment.
- Care for animals and plant life because they were created by God.

Reasons

Christianity teaches that after death, humans will be judged by God for their actions whilst on Earth. This includes how they have looked after the Earth. The Bible shows that God will be angry with those who have ruined or damaged the environment.

Christians believe that conservation of the environment is vital. **however**, they also accept that **people** are the most important of God's creations.

Now try this

1 What is meant by **creation**? (a, 2 marks)

2 Explain how Christian teachings encourage people to care for the world. (c, 8 marks)

Take time to explain your ideas fully, developing them as much as possible by giving clear reasons and examples.

Muslim teachings on stewardship and attitudes to the environment

Muslims believe Allah created the world and gave it to mankind as a gift. They believe they have a duty of **stewardship** to care for the world. They take this responsibility very seriously.

Muslim teachings

- Allah put humans in charge of his creation so Muslims should **respect** this gift.
- Adam, the first human, was made as a *khalifah* or **caretaker** of the Earth. All humans have been given this responsibility.
- The balance of the Earth must be maintained. Allah created everything to have **unity** and all is dependent on everything else in the world.
- All Muslims are part of the *ummah* (worldwide Muslim family) and should look after the world for future generations, making sure natural resources are shared equally.
- Animals are part of Allah's creation. Because humans are *khalifahs* they should treat animals with respect.
- On the Day of Judgement, Allah will **judge** everyone on how they have lived their lives, including whether they have taken care of the world.

The effect on Muslim attitudes to the environment

Islam teaches that all Muslims should look after the world and share natural resources. They do this by:

✔ Supporting environmental organisations and charities.

✔ Recycling and reducing energy use.

✔ Planting trees and crops and using them for the good of others.

✘ Not overusing the Earth's resources.

✘ Sharing the Earth's resources more equally.

✘ Not damaging the natural environment.

✘ Avoiding waste and pollution.

Now try this

1 'It is the responsibility of every human to care for the environment'. In your answer you should refer to at least one religion.

(i) Do you agree? Give reasons for your answer. **(d, 3 marks)**

(ii) Give reasons why some people may disagree with you. **(3 marks)**

You must give at least one religious reason in your answer. You could try to answer this question using Islam.

Had a look ☐ Nearly there ☐ Nailed it! ☐

Medical treatment for infertility

Infertility means not being able to have children. There are a wide range of medical treatments available today to treat infertility but some are **controversial** and raise issues.

Types of medical treatment for infertility

Artificial insemination by husband/partner (AIH)	The husband or partner's sperm is medically put into the mother's womb.
In-vitro fertilisation (IVF)	An egg is taken from the mother and fertilised in a test tube with the sperm and then placed back in her womb.
Artificial insemination by donor (AID)	The sperm of a donor, usually unknown to the couple, is medically put into the mother's womb.
Egg donation	The husband/partner's sperm is used to fertilise a donor egg in a test tube and then put in the woman's womb.
Embryo donation	Both sperm and eggs are provided by anonymous donors then placed in the woman's womb.
Surrogacy	Another woman will carry the baby to full term, either using the couple's sperm and egg or that of a donor.

Issues

- Fertility treatments are very expensive.
- There are no guarantees that procedures will work and many attempts may be needed.
- Fertility drugs have uncomfortable side effects.
- The couple's relationship may be put under great strain because of treatment.
- Donor sperm or eggs can cause conflict or problems bonding with the child.
- Should children know their biological parents?
- Surrogacy can cause problems if the surrogate bonds with the child.

Fertility issues can be very distressing.

Now try this

1 What is meant by **infertility**? **(a, 2 marks)**

2 'Fertility treatment is a waste of money because there is no guarantee a couple will have a child'. In your answer you should refer to at least one religion.

(i) Do you agree? Give reasons for your opinion. **(d, 3 marks)**

(ii) Give reasons why some people may disagree with you. **(3 marks)**

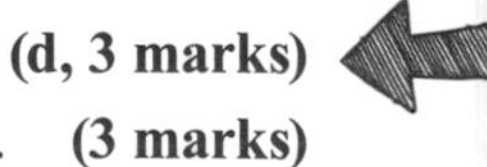

Make sure the two different parts of your answer give clearly different views and that you make your own opinion clear. For example, 'I agree because…' or 'I disagree because…'.

Christian attitudes to fertility treatments

Christians are **divided** in their views over medical treatment for infertility.

Christian responses to infertility:

- Some may accept it is God's plan for them not to have children.
- Some may choose to adopt children.
- Some may direct their parental skills in a different way through a school, charity or Church work.
- Some may choose to explore fertility treatments.

Different Christian attitudes to fertility treatment

AGAINST	REASONS
No one has 'a right' to have children if this is not God's will. Treatments where fertilisation takes place outside the womb involve masturbation, which is a sin. Where embryos are created, usually those not used are destroyed. Some feel that this is murder. Many are against treatments where donated sperm or eggs are used because this is seen as adultery. Most do not accept surrogacy.	God has a plan for everyone and this should be respected. He intended children to be created naturally through sex between a married couple. Surrogacy and donated sperm or eggs bring a third person into the relationship (seen as adultery). Also, destroying unused embryos is against the Christian principle of sanctity of life.

FOR	
It allows infertile couples to experience the joy of having children, as God intended. It depends on the situation and may be more acceptable for married childless couples. God gave humans the knowledge to create children artificially.	Christianity teaches that God commanded humans to 'be fruitful and multiply' (Genesis 1:28). Fertility treatment is also a way of loving your neighbour and follows the Golden Rule of treating others as you would want to be treated.

Now try this

1 Explain why some Christians support infertility treatment and others oppose it. **(c, 8 marks)**

2 'Couples who cannot have children should be entitled to infertility treatments free of charge'. You must refer to at least one religion in your answer.

(i) Do you agree? Give reasons for your opinion. **(d, 3 marks)**

(ii) Give reasons why some people may disagree with you. **(3 marks)**

Make sure you read the question carefully. This question asks you to explain both sides of Christian attitudes to infertility treatment, rather than just one.

Muslim attitudes to fertility treatments

Muslims are expected to have children because they believe it is what Allah wants. Most Muslims believe help should be given to couples who cannot have children naturally. Some types of treatment for infertility are **acceptable** because:

1. Infertility is seen as a disease so it is okay to try and find a cure.

2. Childbirth and childrearing are **important** family commitments.
3. Having children brings the couple closer together.
4. The role and status of a Muslim woman in society and the family involves her ability to have children.

NOT ALLOWED	REASONS
Some Muslims believe that if Allah does not want a couple to have a child, they should accept it and not have treatment.	Muslims will try to act in the way Allah wishes.
Most Muslims disagree with using donor sperm or eggs.	It is seen as adultery. All children have the right to know their natural parents.
All Muslims believe that surrogacy is wrong.	It is seen as adultery. It is believed the woman who gives birth is the mother of the child.

ALLOWED

In-vitro fertilisation (IVF) and artificial insemination by the husband are permitted.	The sperm and egg used are from the married couple. Embryos destroyed during IVF are 14 days old and Islam teaches the soul does not enter the foetus until 120 days. God has given humans the knowledge and ability to create humans in this way. If treatment does not work, Muslims believe this is the wish of Allah.

EXAM ALERT!

Make sure you learn your key words really well as the different types of fertility treatment can easily be confused.

Students have struggled with this topic in recent exams – **be prepared!** ResultsPlus

Now try this

1 Choose one religion other than Christianity and explain why some of its followers accept infertility treatment and some do not. **(c, 8 marks)**

Try to answer this question from an Islamic point of view. Aim to explain clearly by giving reasons (using phrases such as 'because'). Remember that the fewer points you offer, the more you need to explain and develop them.

Transplant surgery

In transplant surgery body parts from one person, dead or alive, are used to replace body parts in someone else. There are both advantages and problems with this issue.

Transplant surgery

The **advantages** of transplant surgery are that people and their loved ones have the opportunity to **help** others after their death because organs are used which would otherwise be wasted. It also offers relief to those who receive transplants and their loved ones.

Ethical problems

- It is an expensive and limited form of treatment.
- How do you decide who receives the transplant? Should it be the person who has been waiting longest, the youngest person or the one with the best match of organ?

Donor Card

I would like to help someone to live after my death.

But don't kill me for my organs

People carry donor cards if they wish to donate their organs to transplant surgery.

Organ donation

Organ donation is voluntary. One person's organs can give life to up to seven different people.

Most organ donations come from dead donors, although liver, kidney and bone marrow transplants can be from a live donor.

Issues raised by organ donation

- It raises questions about when a person is actually considered 'dead'.
- Who should get the organ when there are not enough for those that need them?
- Family members may feel pressurised into donating the organs of a loved one.
- Should a person be kept alive or allowed to die purely for organ donation?
- There are not enough donor organs for those requiring organs.
- Should humans be using organs from animals?

Now try this

1 Do you think people should be paid to donate their organs? Give **two** reasons for your point of view. **(b, 4 marks)**

2 Explain why transplant surgery is important. **(c, 8 marks)**

Try to write a new paragraph for each of your reasons/explanations. This will make it easy to read back through your answer to make sure it is well argued, coherent (clear and organised) and that your spelling, punctuation and grammar are good.

Had a look ☐ Nearly there ☐ Nailed it! ☐

Christian attitudes to transplant surgery

Most Christians have no moral problems with donating organs because it is seen as a charitable act. Some, however, are opposed to it.

Reasons Christians agree with transplant surgery

Be an organ donor
Give your heart to Jesus!

Most Christians believe that transplant surgery should always be done in a responsible way and decisions about who should receive organs should not be based on age, sex or social status.

- ✔ For some, it raises no problems for the afterlife because a body is not needed in Heaven.
- ✔ Organ donation is a **loving** and **charitable** act that follows the teaching of Jesus to love one another.
- ✔ It is a way of people showing gratitude to God for the gift of life.

- ✔ Some believe organ donation is a matter of personal conscience.
- ✔ Other Christians feel that organ donation is a **positive action** and are encouraged to be donors.
- ✔ Some argue that the donor must be pronounced dead before donation.

Reasons Christians might disagree

Some Christians are opposed to transplant surgery because:

- ✘ It goes against the **sanctity of life** teaching because people should not 'play God'.
- ✘ It interferes with God's plan for every human being.
- ✘ The organs are part of a person created by God and it would be wrong to replace part of God's **creation**.
- ✘ Some may argue that organs shouldn't be replaced if a person has deliberately caused the damage to themselves, for example through alcohol.

To be successful on these (a) questions make sure you learn your key words really well.

Now try this

1 What is meant by **organ donation**? **(a, 2 marks)**

2 Do you think all religious people should donate their organs? Give two reasons for your point of view. **(b, 4 marks)**

Try to develop both of your reasons. You can do this by giving an example or a scriptural quote.

Muslim attitudes to transplant surgery

Muslims believe that decisions concerning organ donation should be left to the **individual**. Some agree with it whereas others disagree.

Different attitudes to transplant surgery

AGAINST	FOR
• The Qur'an teaches that the body should be buried soon after death and should not be interfered with. • Muslims believe the body will be **resurrected** on the last day and the organs will therefore be needed. This may also be the case for live donations. • It goes against the **sanctity of life** because only God should give and take life.	• Some Muslims argue that organ donation is okay if done to **save** the life of others because this is what Allah would wish. • Live donations are less controversial because people can survive with one kidney, for example. So the resurrection would be unaffected. • Many Muslims would allow living donor transplants to close relatives.

Islamic authorities

In 1995, the Muslim Law (Shari'ah) Council UK issued guidance on organ donation stating:

- The Council supports organ transplants to alleviate pain or save life.
- Muslims may carry donor cards.
- In the absence of a donor card, the next of kin may give permission for the organs of a loved one to be used to save other people's lives.

Now try this

1. 'Religion should have no say in whether a person chooses to donate his or her organs'. In your answer you should refer to at least one religion.
   (i) Do you agree? Give reasons for your opinion. **(d, 3 marks)**
   (ii) Give reasons why some people may disagree with you. **(3 marks)**
2. Choose one religion other than Christianity and explain why some of its followers may support organ donation and others may not. **(c, 8 marks)**

Make sure you take time to read the question and understand what the statement means so that you can answer the question successfully.

Had a look ☐ Nearly there ☐ Nailed it! ☐

Key words

It is important that you learn the key words for each topic. This is so you can explain what they mean for (a) type questions and use the key words in your answers to other questions to explain ideas fully.

Key words	Definitions
artificial insemination	injecting semen into the uterus by artificial means
conservation	protecting and preserving natural resources and the environment
creation	the act of creating the universe or the universe which has been created
embryo	a fertilised egg in the first eight weeks after conception
environment	the surroundings in which plants and animals live and on which they depend to live
global warming	the increase in the temperature of the Earth's atmosphere (thought to be caused by the greenhouse effect)
infertility	not being able to have children
in-vitro fertilisation (IVF)	the method of fertilising a human egg in a test tube
natural resources	naturally occurring materials, such as oil and fertile land, which can be used by humans
organ donation	giving organs to be used in transplant surgery
stewardship	looking after something so it can be passed on to the next generation
surrogacy	an arrangement whereby a woman bears a child on behalf of another woman **or** where an egg is donated and fertilised by the husband through IVF and then implanted into the wife's uterus

Why do wars occur?

War is an armed conflict between two or more nations. There are many causes of war and often it is a **combination** of factors that leads to war.

Causes of war

- Self defence – to defend your country if attacked
- Economics/natural resources – water, land, oil
- Fear
- National pride
- Fighting against injustice and aggression (unprovoked attacks)
- Racial or ethnic hatred
- Protecting people from persecution and exploitation – where those weaker are taken advantage of

Darfur, 2003–2007

A civil war between the Sudanese army (supported by the government and an Arab military group, the Janjaweed) and a number of different mainly non-Arab groups (including the Sudan Liberation Movement and the Justice and Equality movement). Sudan is now split into two countries, Sudan and The Republic of South Sudan, but the situation is still unsettled.

Economic/environmental

Food and water shortages due to drought and increasing desertification forced many people to move south onto farmland already owned by others struggling to survive. Farmers were also growing cash crops reducing the amount of land available to grow food.

Long-standing ethnic hatred

Both sides have a history of long-standing disputes over religious and ethnic issues. The government was accused of persecuting non-Arabs.

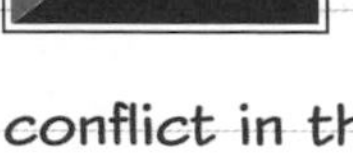

National pride

The conflict in Darfur was part of a wider conflict in the Sudan. Some parts of the anti-government forces wanted the south of Sudan to be ruled as an independent country. The government wished it to remain as one country.

Remote location

This area is remote with poor transport and communication links. When trouble began, it took a long time for other countries to find out. By the time the international community found out, thousands were already dead or had lost their homes.

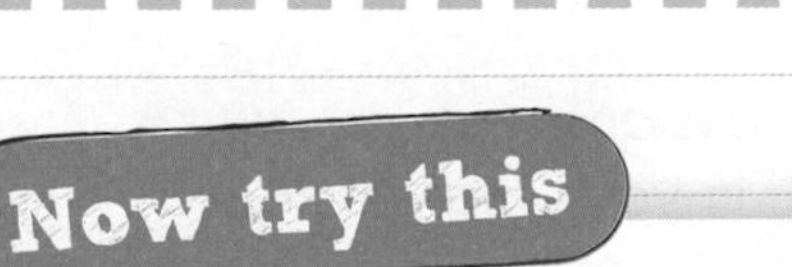

1 Explain why wars happen, using examples from at least one current conflict. **(c, 8 marks)**

You could use the information on this page to include Darfur as an example to help you explain why wars happen.

Had a look ☐ Nearly there ☐ Nailed it! ☐

The United Nations and world peace

The United Nations (UN) is an international body set up after the Second World War to promote world peace and cooperation. There are 192 member nations who meet regularly at the UN Headquarters in New York.

The UN

- Uses conflict resolution (bringing fighting to a peaceful conclusion) and reconciliation (bringing people opposed to each other together).
- Range of **methods** used: arms control and disarmament to reduce numbers of weapons of mass destruction, peace talks, trade restrictions, sending peacekeeping forces and military action.
- Concerned with issues that will have a long-term impact on world peace – fighting against poverty, campaigning for human rights, solving conflict issues.
- Basic aim is to achieve world peace – the ending of war throughout the world.
- Has experienced both **success** (achieving peace and reducing human rights abuses) and **failure** (too late to prevent mass killing in Darfur).

Case study: Darfur

Negotiation

After the conflict became known, the UN negotiated between the two sides. The Sudanese government and the UN formed an agreement to stop the conflict. The government failed to follow the agreement. Various peace deals were signed and broken but the UN had some success in getting both sides to talk.

Sanctions

Several countries stopped trading with Sudan. The UN threatened sanctions (e.g. to stop Sudan trading in oil). This achieved some response from the Sudan government to work with the UN.

Peacekeeping forces

A small African Union peacekeeping force was allowed into Darfur in August 2004. Not until 2007 was an agreed peacekeeping force from the UN and African Union allowed in. This is ongoing and has had some success in protecting civilians but has also come under attack from both sides.

4 Success / failure?

The UN has at least managed to stem the number and frequency of killings and organised more peace talks. However, peace has still not yet been achieved and intervention was too late to prevent mass killing in Darfur.

Now try this

1 What is the **United Nations**? **(a, 2 marks)**

2 Explain how the United Nations works for world peace using a relevant example. **(c, 8 marks)**

All 'explain' questions require you to go into depth in your answer. Try to use phrases such as 'because' to help you explain, and to support your answer make sure you use an example of the UN's work that you have studied.

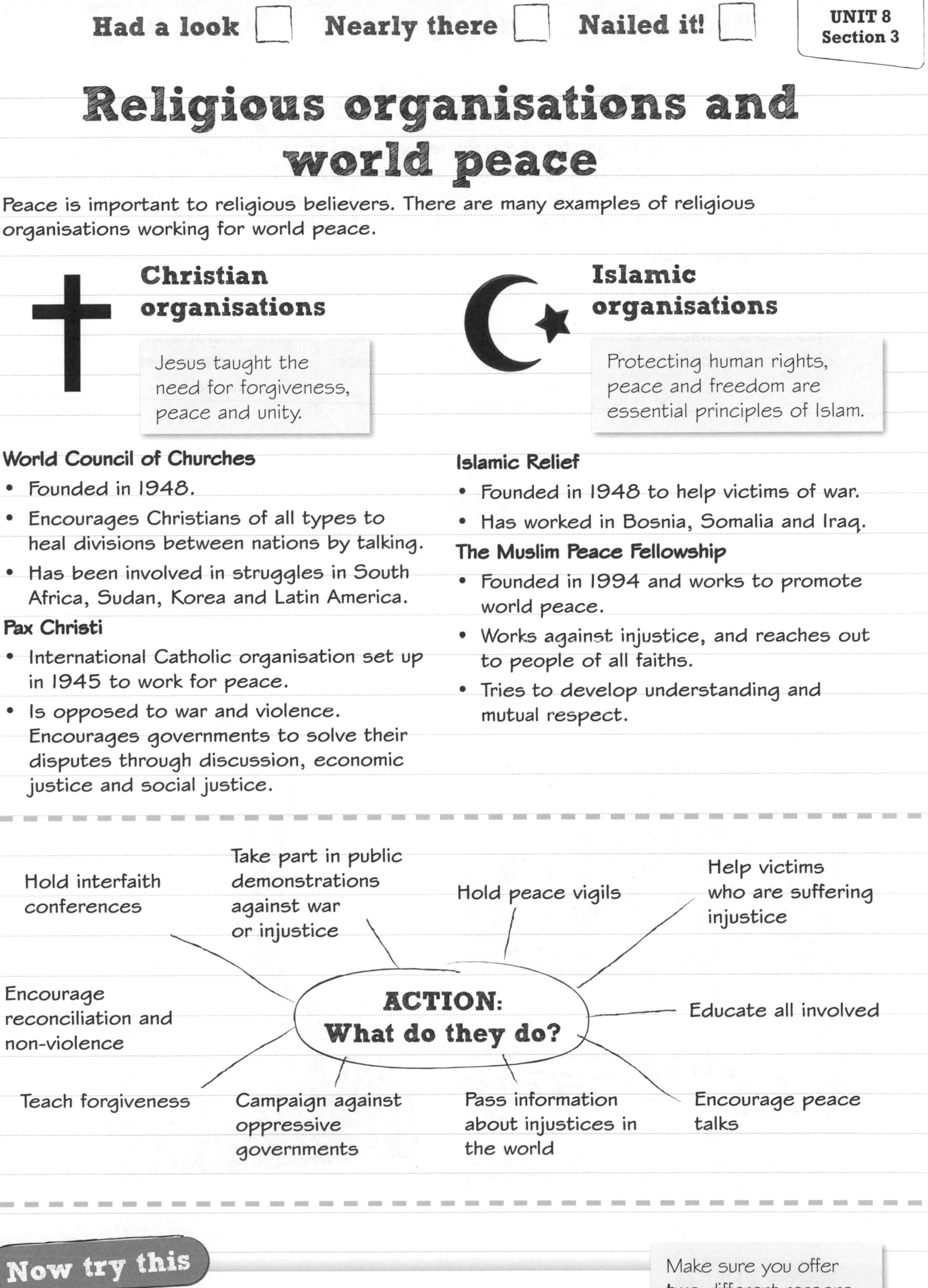

Religious organisations and world peace

Peace is important to religious believers. There are many examples of religious organisations working for world peace.

Christian organisations

Jesus taught the need for forgiveness, peace and unity.

World Council of Churches

- Founded in 1948.
- Encourages Christians of all types to heal divisions between nations by talking.
- Has been involved in struggles in South Africa, Sudan, Korea and Latin America.

Pax Christi

- International Catholic organisation set up in 1945 to work for peace.
- Is opposed to war and violence. Encourages governments to solve their disputes through discussion, economic justice and social justice.

Islamic organisations

Protecting human rights, peace and freedom are essential principles of Islam.

Islamic Relief

- Founded in 1948 to help victims of war.
- Has worked in Bosnia, Somalia and Iraq.

The Muslim Peace Fellowship

- Founded in 1994 and works to promote world peace.
- Works against injustice, and reaches out to people of all faiths.
- Tries to develop understanding and mutual respect.

ACTION: What do they do?

- Hold interfaith conferences
- Take part in public demonstrations against war or injustice
- Hold peace vigils
- Help victims who are suffering injustice
- Encourage reconciliation and non-violence
- Educate all involved
- Teach forgiveness
- Campaign against oppressive governments
- Pass information about injustices in the world
- Encourage peace talks

Now try this

1 What is **forgiveness**? **(a, 2 marks)**

2 Do you think religious organisations should do more for world peace? Give two reasons for your point of view. **(b, 4 marks)**

Make sure you offer **two** different reasons to support your opinion. You can also develop each reason by giving an example.

Had a look ☐ Nearly there ☐ Nailed it! ☐

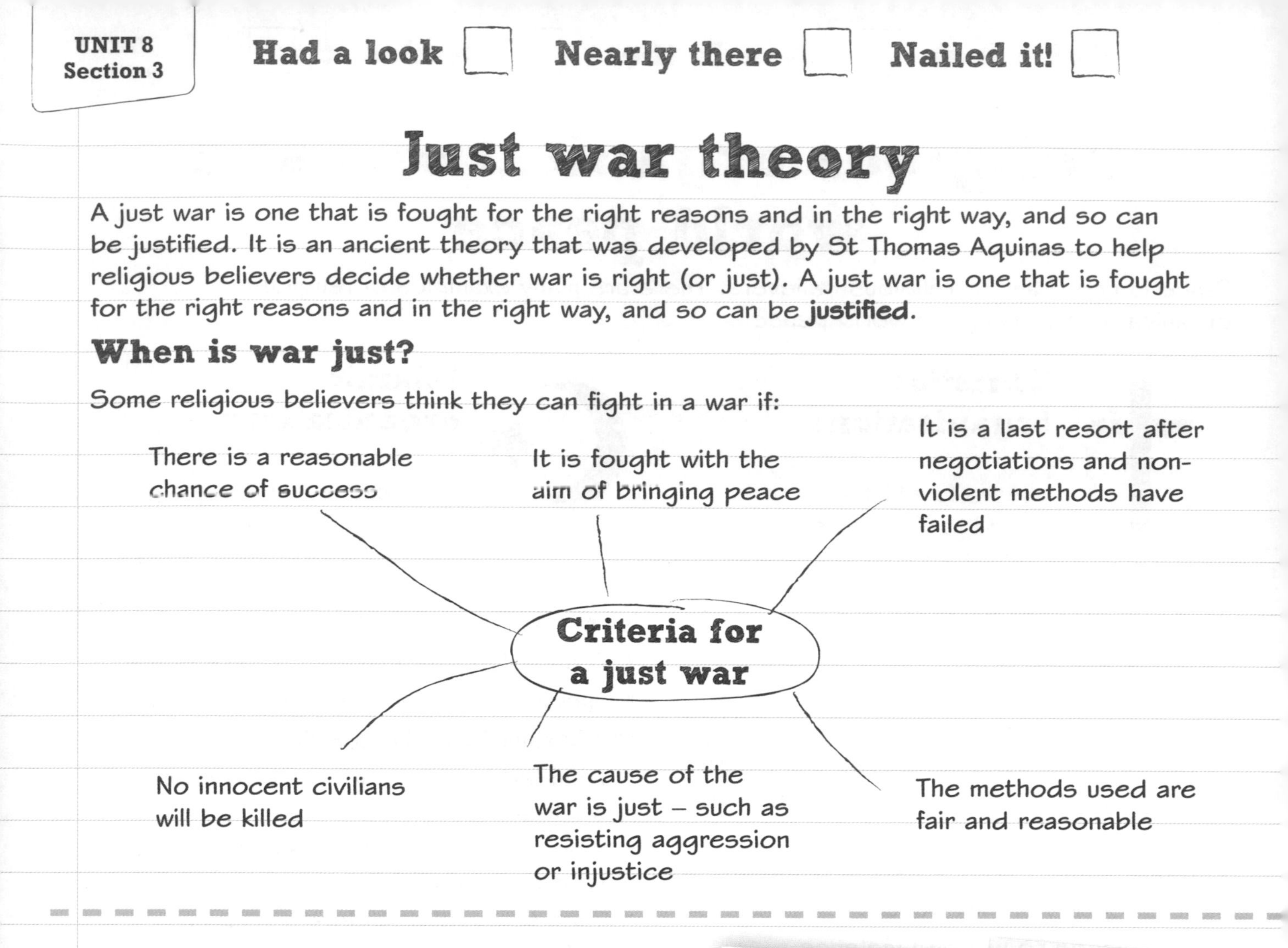

Just war theory

A just war is one that is fought for the right reasons and in the right way, and so can be justified. It is an ancient theory that was developed by St Thomas Aquinas to help religious believers decide whether war is right (or just). A just war is one that is fought for the right reasons and in the right way, and so can be **justified**.

When is war just?

Some religious believers think they can fight in a war if:

Issues with just war

Both sides in a war may claim their cause is 'just'. For example, in the Second World War, Hitler claimed the Nazis were right and just in their fight.

Just war theory has been manipulated by leaders to justify their actions and claim that they have fought in the name of God.

In the Iraq war the USA claimed they invaded for the force of good, but al-Qaeda claimed they fought in the name of Allah.

Now try this

1 What is **just war** theory? **(a, 2 marks)**

2 Explain why just war theory is important. **(c, 8 marks)**

When you explain just war theory, remember to explain how the criteria helps to justify a war.

Christian attitudes to war

The Bible teaches Christians to find **peace** and **reconciliation** with their enemies, although attitudes to war continue to **differ**.

Bible teachings

- The Bible has a message of peace.
- One of the titles given to Jesus was 'Prince of Peace'.

'Blessed are the peacemakers...' (Matthew 5:9).
'...If someone strikes you on the right cheek, turn to him the other also'. (Matthew 5:39).
'Love your enemies...' (Matthew 5:44).
'For all who draw the sword will die by the sword' (Matthew 26:52).

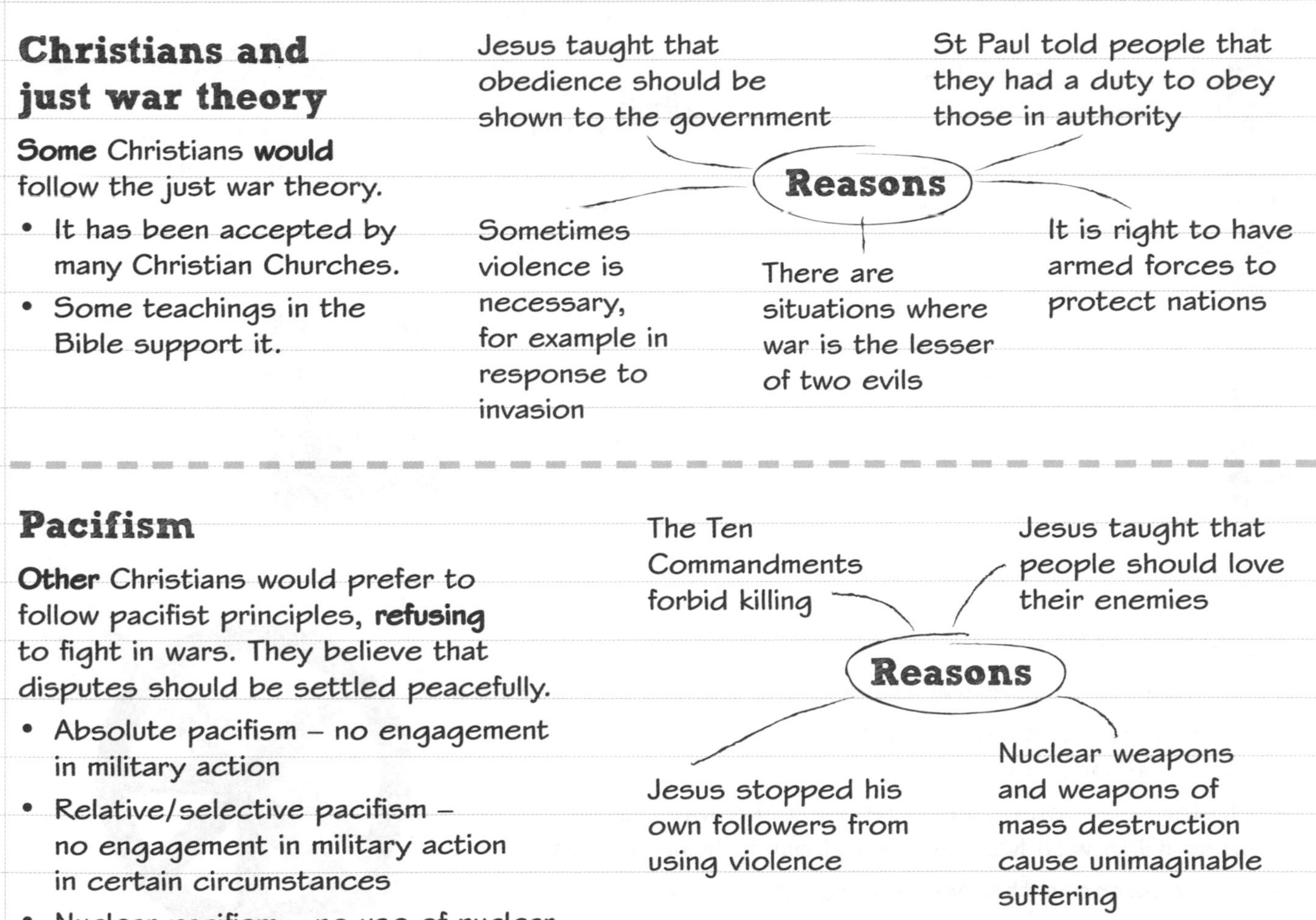

Christians and just war theory

Some Christians **would** follow the just war theory.

- It has been accepted by many Christian Churches.
- Some teachings in the Bible support it.

Reasons

- Jesus taught that obedience should be shown to the government
- St Paul told people that they had a duty to obey those in authority
- Sometimes violence is necessary, for example in response to invasion
- There are situations where war is the lesser of two evils
- It is right to have armed forces to protect nations

Pacifism

Other Christians would prefer to follow pacifist principles, **refusing** to fight in wars. They believe that disputes should be settled peacefully.

- Absolute pacifism – no engagement in military action
- Relative/selective pacifism – no engagement in military action in certain circumstances
- Nuclear pacifism – no use of nuclear weapons

Reasons

- The Ten Commandments forbid killing
- Jesus taught that people should love their enemies
- Jesus stopped his own followers from using violence
- Nuclear weapons and weapons of mass destruction cause unimaginable suffering

Now try this

1 Explain why some Christians will fight in a war and some will not. **(c, 8 marks)**

Plan your answer carefully to ensure you show both the reasons why some Christians will fight and why others will not. Try to start a new paragraph for each point you make and explain each one fully.

Muslim attitudes to war

'Islam' means 'peace' although the Qur'an teaches that this will not be easy. 'Jihad' is an Islamic term meaning 'struggle' and there are two types, lesser and greater jihad. However, many Muslims actually oppose war.

Lesser jihad

Lesser jihad is a just war theory. It is a physical struggle or war. Although the Qur'an teaches peace, there are **some** circumstances in which the use of violence is allowed.

1. If fought for a just cause – to defend Islam or injustice.
2. As a last resort.
3. If it is authorised by Muslim authority.
4. The minimum amount of suffering is caused.
5. Ends when enemy surrenders.
6. Innocent civilians are not attacked.
7. When the aim is to restore peace and freedom.

Greater jihad

This is the struggle Muslims face within themselves in order to make them better Muslims and bring them closer to God. For example, studying the Qur'an, doing good deeds, attending mosque and fighting greed and envy.

Under these rules Muslims **should** fight because:

- The Qur'an teaches that it is right if attacked.
- Muhammad fought in wars and taught that Muslims should fight in just wars.
- The Qur'an teaches that anyone killed in a just war goes straight to Heaven.

Against war

Some Muslims believe war is **never** the right choice because:

✗ Peace and reconciliation is at the heart of Islam and the teachings of the Qur'an.
✗ Modern weapons cannot be used in a way that is compatible with Muslim rules about fighting in a war.
✗ Non-violence is the only way to achieve peace.
✗ Violence only leads to more violence.

1. Do you think it is ever right to go to war? Give two reasons for your point of view. **(b, 4 marks)**
2. Choose one religion other than Christianity and explain its teachings on war. **(c, 8 marks)**

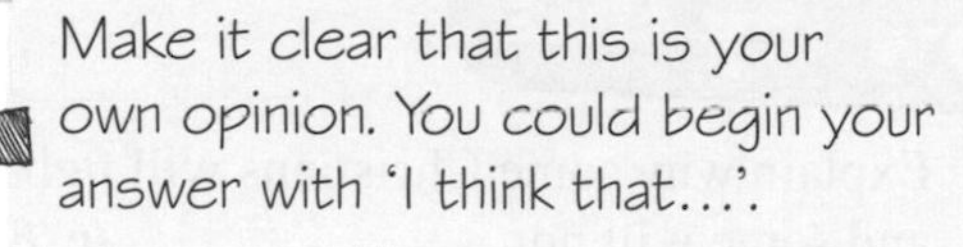

Christian attitudes to bullying

Conflict can also be between people. One type of conflict is bullying which can be either physical or verbal. Christians are **opposed** to all forms of bullying.

What is bullying?

Intimidating or frightening people weaker than yourself by:

- Physically harming or attacking someone.
- Stealing or damaging someone else's property.

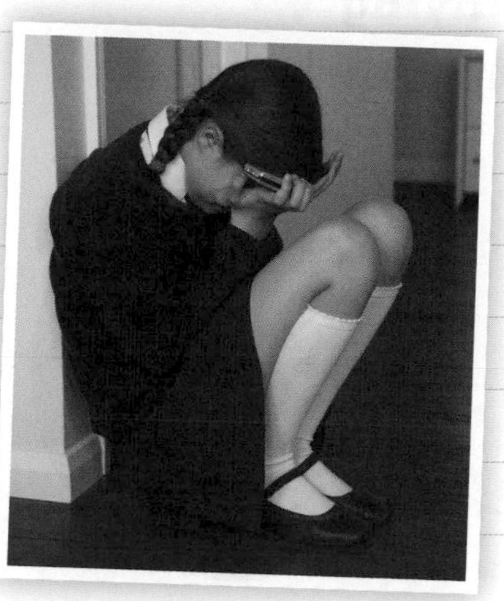

- Accusing people of things they have not done to get them into trouble.
- Calling people names.
- Cyberbullying.

Reasons

The reasons why some people bully others might include having problems at home, problems with family members, wanting to look tough, or they dislike themselves and take it out on others. Bullies may themselves have been victims of bullying.

The Samaritans

The Samaritans are a well-known UK charity that offers telephone support to people suffering from bullying. Many Christians are volunteers for the Samaritans.

SAMARITANS

Christian attitudes to bullying

All Christians believe bullying is wrong because:

- Violence without cause is **against** Christian teachings.
- Every individual was created by God in his image so bullying is mistreating God's creation.
- Jesus taught that people should **love** one another and treat others as they would like to be treated.
- Everyone should be treated with **respect** and the weak and vulnerable deserve protection.
- The Bible teaches that God will take action against cruel behaviour.
- God will **judge** humans after death on the way they have lived. If they have bullied others, he will not be pleased.

Now try this

1 'Bullies deserve sympathy not punishment'.
In your answer you should refer to at least one religion.

(i) Do you agree? Give reasons for your opinion. **(d, 3 marks)**

(ii) Give reasons why some people might disagree with you. **(3 marks)**

Try to give up to **three** reasons for your opinion for each part of your answer, and explain each one clearly. You could give an example to help support your answer.

Had a look ☐ Nearly there ☐ Nailed it! ☐

Muslim attitudes to bullying

Like Christians, Muslims are opposed to all forms of bullying.

Muslim attitudes to bullying

Muslims are opposed to all forms of bullying because...

Islam teaches aggression or violence without just cause is **wrong**

Every person was created by Allah and it is wrong to abuse any part of his creation

Islam teaches that Muslims should work to end injustice and cruelty

Muhammad taught that Muslims should **protect** and help the weak and vulnerable

All Muslims believe that on the last day they will be **judged** by Allah on the way they have lived their lives

People who can help

Muslim parents and Muslim organisations may support organisations that help the victims of bullying because the Qur'an teaches that Muslims should work together to challenge wrongdoing.

Christians are also likely to support these organisations.

ChildLine:

- is a free confidential 24-hour helpline for children and young people
- offers help of trained counsellors to resolve many different problems.

ChildLine has offered advice and guidelines to schools to tackle bullying:

- get everyone in school to tackle bullying
- put anti-bullying posters up and educate everyone about the problem of bullying
- make sure staff are around at breaktimes when most bullying happens
- set up peer counselling schemes to provide support.

Kidscape:

- was founded in 1984 by Dr Michele Elliot
- aims to teach children about personal safety and how to deal with issues such as bullying.

Now try this

1 Do you think we should do more to stop bullying in schools? Give two reasons for your point of view. **(b, 4 marks)**

2 Explain why the followers of one religion other than Christianity may be against bullying. **(c, 8 marks)**

Religious conflict within families

Conflicts within families are usual and happen for many reasons. Religious believers offer teachings on how to deal with family conflict but religion can also be a source of conflict.

Common causes of family conflict

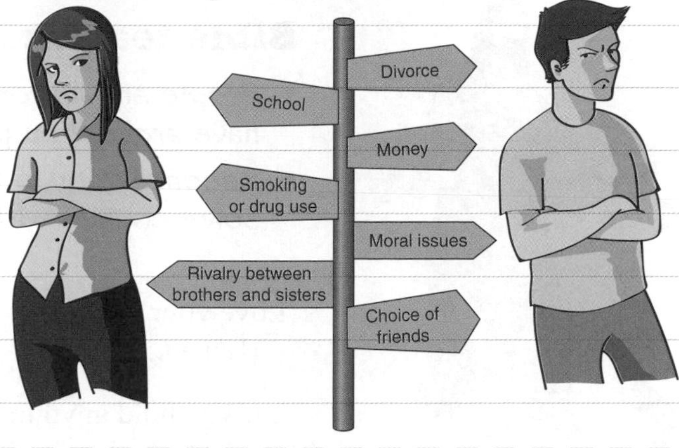

Causes of conflict in religious families

Here are some other issues that could cause conflict within **religious** families:

- **Social behaviour** – drinking alcohol, socialising with members of the opposite sex.
- **Moral issues** – cohabiting with a partner or choosing to have an abortion.
- **Jobs and careers** – certain careers could conflict with religious teachings.
- **Choice of boyfriend/girlfriend** – especially if they are from another faith.
- **Raising children** – society and times have changed and older generations may hold different views.

Religion itself can be a source of conflict within families. A child with a religious upbringing may convert to a different faith or decide not to follow any faith. Or a child of atheist parents may choose to follow a religion.

Christianity

Christianity teaches that:

- children should honour their parents as stated in the Ten Commandments
- parents should care for their children and support them.

Islam

Islam teaches that:

- no child should cause harm to their parents and parents should care for their children
- Muslims should obey their parents, even in adulthood and respect the wisdom they offer.

Now try this

1 Do you think there is more conflict in a religious family? Give two reasons for your point of view. **(b, 4 marks)**

2 Explain why religion may be a source of conflict within families. **(c, 8 marks)**

Make sure you give specific examples to support the **two** reasons you give to show your view.

Had a look ☐ Nearly there ☐ Nailed it! ☐

Christian teachings on forgiveness and reconciliation

Forgiveness is to stop blaming someone for what they have done and reconciliation is the process of bringing people back together. Christianity teaches that this is the way to resolve conflict.

Jesus

Jesus died on the cross to bring forgiveness and reconciliation between humanity and God.

Christians should forgive others and God will help them to do this even when it is difficult.

Bible teachings

- People should forgive those they have argued/fought with.
- Reconciliation is the best way to solve conflict with family and friends.

'Love your enemies...'
(Luke 6:27).

'...if you hold anything against anyone, forgive him...'
(Mark 11:25).

Are some things unforgiveable?

- **Murder:** Anthony Walker, 18, was murdered in a racially motivated attack in 2005.
- **But** his Christian parents spoke after the murderers were sent to prison saying they stood by their Christian teachings of forgiveness.

Some Christians believe that with the love of God **everything** is forgivable. Christians believe that if they don't forgive, God will not forgive them.

Other Christians argue that if the conflict was about a religious or moral issue where the Bible had a definite teaching, then there can be no reconciliation.

Now try this

1 Do you think it is always possible to forgive others? Give two reasons for your point of view. **(b, 4 marks)**

2 'Religious people should always forgive'. In your answer you should refer to at least one religion.

(i) Do you agree? Give reasons for your opinion. **(d, 3 marks)**

(ii) Give reasons why some people may disagree with you. **(3 marks)**

Identify which religion or religions you are going to refer to and ensure that at least one of your reasons is a religious one. Try to also be very clear about whether you agree or disagree, for example 'I disagree that religious people should always forgive, because…'.

Muslim teachings on forgiveness and reconciliation

Islam teaches that conflict should be resolved by forgiveness and reconciliation.

Muslim teachings

Conflicts should be resolved using the ideas of **forgiveness** and **reconciliation**.

Muhammad taught people should forgive and be reconciled with those who have offended them.

On the Day of Judgement it is believed Allah will show mercy and forgiveness to those who have done the same towards others.

The Qur'an teaches that forgiveness and reconciliation are important:

'If a person forgives and makes reconciliation, his reward is due from God' (Surah 42:40).

One name given to Allah is 'the Compassionate and Merciful' showing Allah **forgives** people and Muslims should too.

Forgiveness and Hajj

On pilgrimage (*Hajj*) to Makkah (Mecca), Muslims climb Jebel al-Rahma (Mount Mercy) on the Plain of Arafat where they will pray for forgiveness. They believe that by doing this, Allah will forgive their sins.

Unforgivable actions

Some actions may **not** be forgivable by Muslims:

✗ Working against Islam.

✗ Freely denying Muslim principles.

✗ Images of Muhammad – In September 2005 a Danish newspaper published cartoon drawings of Muhammad that were considered deeply offensive to Islam and unforgiveable.

Now try this

1 What is **forgiveness**? **(a, 2 marks)**

2 What is **reconciliation**? **(a, 2 marks)**

To do well on these (a) type questions, make sure you learn your key words.

Key words

It is important that you learn the key words for each topic. This is so you can explain what they mean for (a) type questions and use the key words in your answers to other questions to explain ideas fully.

Key words	Definitions
aggression	attacking without being provoked
bullying	intimidating/frightening people weaker than yourself
conflict resolution	bringing a fight or struggle to a peaceful conclusion
exploitation	taking advantage of a weaker group
forgiveness	stopping blaming someone and/or pardoning them for what they have done wrong
just war	a war which is fought for the right reasons and in a right way
pacifism	the belief that all disputes should be settled by peaceful means
reconciliation	bringing together people who were opposed to each other
respect	treating a person or their feelings with consideration
the United Nations	an international body set up to promote world peace and cooperation
weapons of mass destruction	weapons which can destroy large areas and numbers of people
world peace	the ending of war throughout the whole world (the basic aim of the United Nations)

The need for law and justice

Law and justice are important to the smooth running of society. Laws are rules made by Parliament, which are enforced by the police and law courts.

Responsibility

Under the law, we must be responsible for our own actions.

Why do we need the law?

- To protect the weak.
- To create peace for everyone to live in.
- To be kept safe from criminals.
- To give guidelines on acceptable behaviour.
- To be able to live without fear.
- To be protected from violence.

Justice	Sin
• Justice comes from the courts because they apply the law fairly. • Justice is the process of allocating rewards or punishments and upholding what is right. • There can be problems if a government passes a law which people think is unfair or unjust.	• A sin is an action that goes against the will of God • Some sins are crimes – for example murder • Other sins such as adultery are not against the law

How are laws made?

1. Proposed law is written out in a document called a Bill. It is introduced and debated in the House of Commons. First reading.
2. Bill is again debated in Parliament. Second reading.
3. Bill is passed to a committee who go through it in detail.
4. Debated again, vote is taken and if in favour of the Bill, it is passed to the House of Lords. Third reading.
5. House of Lords debate and vote on the Bill.
6. If passed, it is sent to the Queen to give it the Royal Assent.
7. The Bill becomes an Act of Parliament and is law.

Now try this

1 What is meant by **the law**? **(a, 2 marks)**
2 What is **a crime**? **(a, 2 marks)**
3 Do you think it is always wrong to break the law? Give two reasons for your point of view. **(b, 4 marks)**

Had a look ☐ Nearly there ☐ Nailed it! ☐

Theories of punishment

In order for the law to work properly, those who break the law have to be punished. There are many theories about the **aims** of punishment. There are also arguments against.

MUGGER GETS FIVE YEARS
A serial mugger was sentenced yesterday at Newtown county court to

Deterrence

Deterrence means to **discourage** someone from doing something that is against the law. Punishment may put someone off doing that action again. Seeing the punishment given might also put someone else off doing the same action.

Retribution

Retribution is the idea that punishment should make criminals **pay** for what they have done wrong. It makes the victim of a crime feel a sense of justice – that the offender 'got what they deserved'.

Theories of punishment

Protection

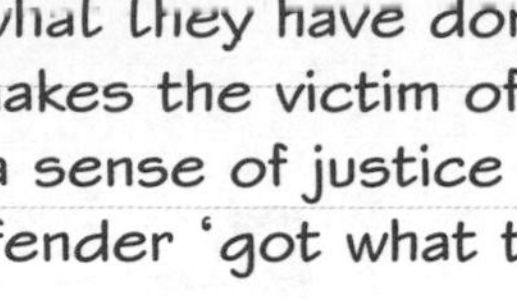

A purpose of punishment is to **protect** society from violent or dangerous criminals by keeping them in prison where they cannot harm others.

Reform

Punishment should help the offender to see what they have done wrong and to change, or reform, so they do not repeat the offence. This may mean providing criminals with education, skills or job training so they become a law-abiding citizen again. This is known as rehabilitation.

In the UK, a person is presumed to be innocent until their guilt is proven by a court.

Arguments against theories of punishment:

- Deterrence doesn't work – nearly half of all criminals reoffend and prisons are full.
- Retribution doesn't always work – some victims feel that criminals do not get severe enough punishments.
- In some serious crimes, it is possible to argue that retribution is never achieved for the victim and their family.
- Reform is seen to go against punishment as it gives criminals more chances.
- Protection only works if criminals are in prison but many are released back into society.
- Some may argue that theories of punishment do not focus on the causes of crime and therefore are irrelevant.

Now try this

1 What is meant by **deterrence**? **(a, 2 marks)**

2 Do you think punishments always achieve their aim? Give two reasons for your point of view. **(b, 4 marks)**

To do well on these (a) type questions make sure you learn your key words thoroughly.

Christians and justice

Justice is important to Christians and is also part of their religious teaching. Many individual Christians and organisations work for justice in the world today.

Christian teachings on justice

- God is **just** and people should behave in the same way.
- Jesus taught that everyone should be treated **fairly** – e.g. the rich helping the poor.
- Jesus taught the Golden Rule – '...do to others what you would have them do to you...' (Matthew 7:12).
- All Christian Churches teach that Christians should behave in a just manner.
- On Judgement Day, God will judge all humans according to how they have behaved. If they have behaved justly they will be rewarded in Heaven.
- It is up to God to judge people and he will forgive those who are truly sorry for what they have done and want to change.

How Christians help

Christians follow Jesus' teachings by:

- Ensuring resources are **shared** equally.
- **Giving** to charity or working in areas of hardship.
- **Campaigning** for governments and organisations to help other nations.
- **Helping** those who are oppressed.

Christian charities

There are many Christian charities that campaign for justice. Two examples are:

christian aid

- Works in areas of poverty.
- Helps those in need and campaigns against injustice and oppression of the poor.
- Seeks to change government policy.
- Campaigns for an end to unjust debts imposed on poorer nations.

- Catholic Fund for Overseas Development.
- Campaigns for justice for the poor.
- Has campaigned against landmines, the debt owed by the third world and for the rich to be more active in helping the poor and oppressed.

Now try this

1 Do you think it is important to work for justice? Give two reasons for your point of view. **(b, 4 marks)**

2 'Religious people should do more to achieve justice in the world.' In your answer you should refer to at least one religion.

(i) Do you agree? Give reasons for your opinion. **(d, 3 marks)**

(ii) Give reasons why some people may disagree with you. **(3 marks)**

Think about beginning with a sentence which gives your opinion and try to make sure that the two parts of your answer are clearly different.

Had a look ☐ Nearly there ☐ Nailed it! ☐

Muslims and justice

Muslims recognise the importance of justice because the Qur'an and Law of God teach that Muslims should act with fairness. Many Muslims **campaign** for peace and justice.

Muslim teachings

- On the Last Day God will reward those who have been just and fair towards others.
- The Qur'an teaches that God wants people to act **fairly** towards everyone.
- Everyone is **equal** under Islamic law.
- Justice is the basis of **charitable giving** in Islam.
- The Shari'ah (Law of God) requires justice for all.
- Prophet Muhammad always acted in a just way.

Shari'ah – Law of God

- Muslims believe they should follow the rules given by Shari'ah law.
- They also believe they must obey the laws of the country they are in, even if they are not Islamic.
- Shari'ah courts have strict rules to ensure they are fair, for example all trials are public so justice is seen to be done.
- Shari'ah also has laws to help society function fairly, for example not charging interest on loans.

Why do Muslims work for justice?

✔ To obey the Qur'an.

✔ To fulfil Shari'ah.

✔ To fulfil the Five Pillars, for example the *Zakah* is a tax of 2.5% on every Muslim income which is given to the poor. Wealth is shared to make society fairer.

✔ Muslims are encouraged to give *Sadaqah* – voluntary charitable donations – and to act charitably towards others.

✔ To please Allah. Muslims believe Allah is watching every action they perform.

Muslim charities

There are many Muslim charities that campaign for justice. Two examples are:

Muslim Aid

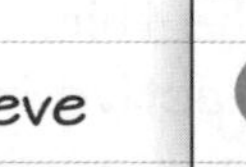

- It works to relieve poverty and secure justice for the poor and oppressed.
- It also aims to get richer nations to help poorer ones and remove oppression.

Islamic Relief

- It seeks to improve the lives of people affected by poverty, wars and natural disasters.
- It also provides emergency food and medical relief.

1 Choose one religion other than Christianity and explain why its followers think justice is important. **(c, 8 marks)**

You could use Islam as your focus in this question. Make sure you explain rather than describe ideas by using phrases such as 'because', and giving examples to support your points.

Non-religious arguments about capital punishment

Capital punishment is also known as the death penalty. There are many strong arguments both **for** and **against** capital punishment.

What is capital punishment?

- It is execution where the life of a condemned prisoner is taken away.
- It was abolished in the UK in 1973, except in cases of treason, and abolished completely in 1998.
- Under the European Convention on Human Rights (1999), execution was abolished throughout the European Union.

EN AMÉRIQUE — EXÉCUTION D'UNE FEMME AUX ÉTATS-UNIS

- Other nations, including some states in the USA, still have the death penalty.
- Methods of execution include hanging, lethal injection, the electric chair, beheading and a firing squad.

Different arguments

FOR

✔ The death penalty is a deterrent to stop people committing crimes.
✔ The value of human life is made clear by taking it away from those who kill others.
✔ It can make people confess their crime in return for a lesser sentence.
✔ Society can rid itself of the most dangerous criminals.
✔ Execution is retribution for taking the life of another and may help the victim's family.
✔ It has a good psychological effect on society who see the idea of bad things happening to bad people as fair.

AGAINST

✘ Those countries that have the death penalty don't seem to have a low crime rate.
✘ Many people have been executed but have later turned out to be innocent.
✘ Some people see execution as 'murder' so it is as bad as the criminal's act.
✘ Human life is special and should not be taken away under any circumstances.
✘ Terrorists who are executed may be seen as heroes and this can further increase terrorist acts.
✘ Some people feel execution is an easier punishment than life imprisonment and the criminal escapes true justice.

Now try this

1 Explain why some non-religious people do not agree with capital punishment. **(c, 8 marks)**

Make sure you read the question carefully. This does **not** require you to discuss religion. Try to explain up to four things that make non-religious people disagree with capital punishment.

Had a look ☐ Nearly there ☐ Nailed it! ☐

Christian attitudes to capital punishment

Christians are divided over their views on capital punishment. They may use both religious and non-religious arguments to support their views.

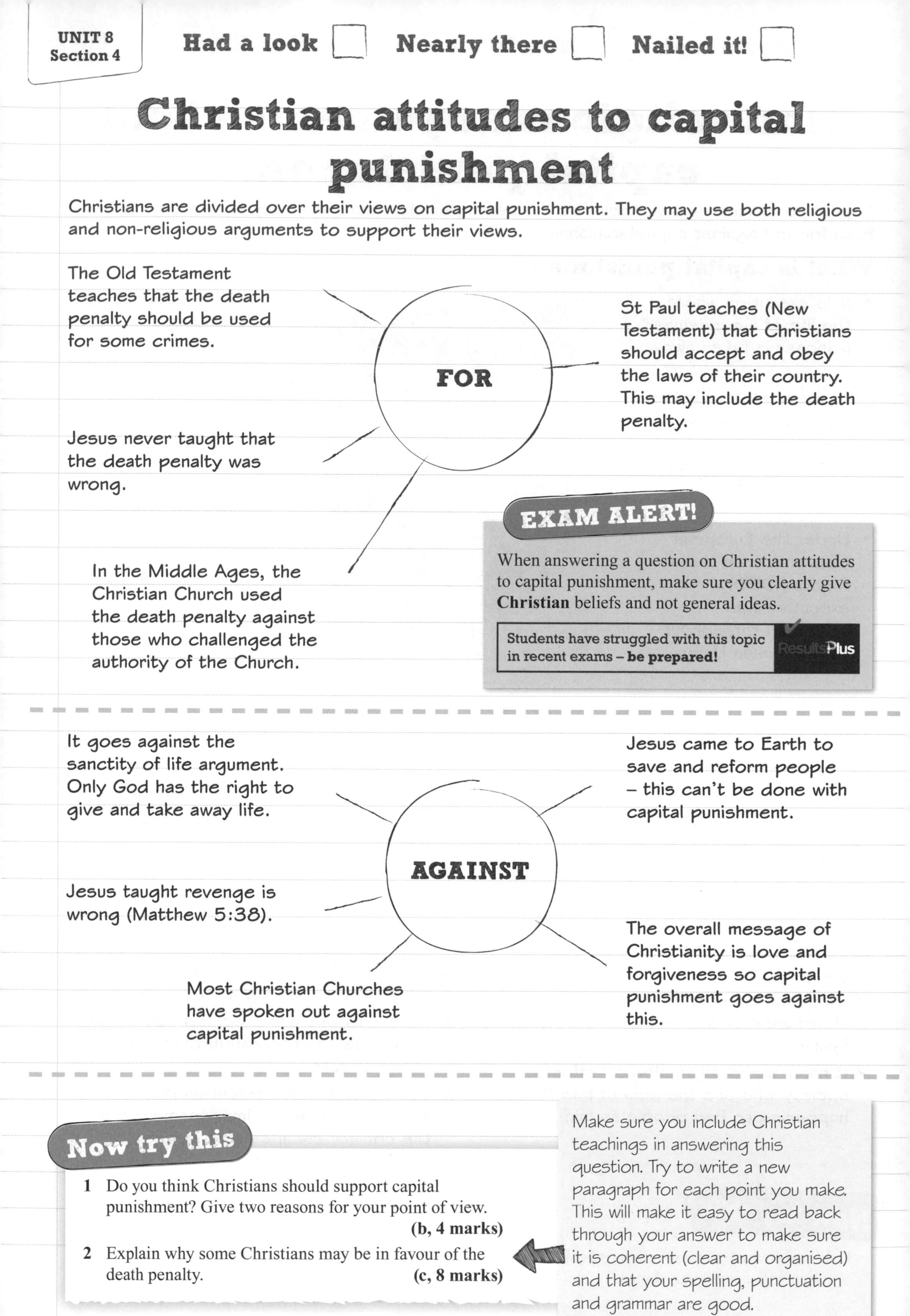

EXAM ALERT!

When answering a question on Christian attitudes to capital punishment, make sure you clearly give **Christian** beliefs and not general ideas.

Students have struggled with this topic in recent exams – **be prepared!**

ResultsPlus

Now try this

1 Do you think Christians should support capital punishment? Give two reasons for your point of view. **(b, 4 marks)**

2 Explain why some Christians may be in favour of the death penalty. **(c, 8 marks)**

Make sure you include Christian teachings in answering this question. Try to write a new paragraph for each point you make. This will make it easy to read back through your answer to make sure it is coherent (clear and organised) and that your spelling, punctuation and grammar are good.

Muslim attitudes to capital punishment

Islam is, in principle, in **favour** of the death penalty for some crimes although there are a **small** number of Muslims who want to abolish it.

Shari'ah

In all countries where Shari'ah law is used, the death penalty can be used.

- The Qur'an teaches that capital punishment can be used for some crimes.
- Crimes that carry the death penalty vary but usually include murder, rape, homosexual acts and apostasy (a Muslim denying or working against Islam).
- According to the Qur'an the death penalty can only be given as a last resort, after a fair trial.
- The criteria for the death penalty are very strict, for example for adultery four people have to testify.
- The victim or their family has to agree to the sentence. If they disagree, another sentence will be given.

Saddam Hussein was a dictator and leader of Iraq. He was found guilty of crimes against humanity in 2006 in Iraq and was sentenced to death.

FOR

✔ The Qur'an says the death penalty can be used for certain crimes such as murder and adultery.

✔ Shari'ah agrees with the Qur'an.

✔ Muhammad made statements suggesting he agreed with the death penalty.

✔ When Muhammad was the ruler of Medina, he sentenced people to death for committing murder.

AGAINST

✘ The scholars of Shari'ah do not agree when or how the death penalty should be applied.

✘ The Qur'an states that capital punishment is one option – it is not compulsory.

✘ Strict conditions given by the Qur'an about capital punishment are often not met.

✘ In some countries Shari'ah has been seen to have oppressed the poor and women who receive the death penalty for adultery.

✘ Some Muslims are persuaded by non-religious arguments against capital punishment.

Now try this

1 'No religious believer should agree with the death penalty'.
You should refer to at least one religion in your answer.

(i) Do you agree? Give reasons for your opinion. **(d, 3 marks)**

(ii) Give reasons why some people may disagree with you. **(3 marks)**

Try to use Islam to help you answer this question. Remember that you can give up to **three** reasons to support each part of your answer but at least one must be religious.

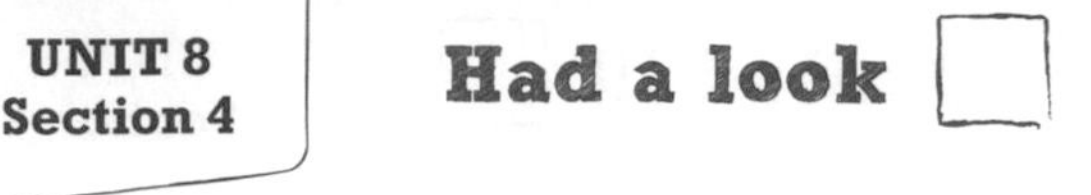

Had a look ☐ Nearly there ☐ Nailed it! ☐

Drugs and alcohol laws

The potential **dangers** of drugs and alcohol means that their sale and consumption is controlled by law in the UK. The law is intended to **protect** consumers and limit the ways drugs and alcohol can be sold.

Drugs

A drug is any chemical you put into your body that changes your mood or the way you feel.

- Some drugs such as alcohol and tobacco can be damaging to a person's health.
- People can become addicted to some drugs.
- Children need protection from some drugs.
- Some drugs cause social problems.
- Some drugs (e.g. antibiotics) can improve health.
- Drugs such as caffeine in tea are seen to be fairly harmless in moderation.

Legal drugs

- Legal drugs, such as some painkillers, are sold under controlled conditions in pharmacies, supermarkets and shops.
- Some are sold over the counter, others only with a prescription.

Illegal drugs

- Illegal drugs are classified according to how dangerous they are.
- Taking or selling Class A drugs carries heavy penalties whereas lower penalties are given for possession or supply of lower class drugs.

Kinds of drugs

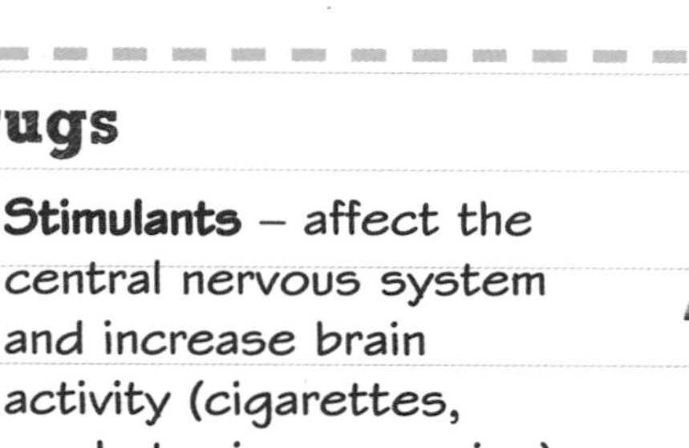

Stimulants – affect the central nervous system and increase brain activity (cigarettes, amphetamines, cocaine)

Hallucinogens – drugs that change your senses and give the impression that things are there when they are not (LSD, magic mushrooms, cannabis)

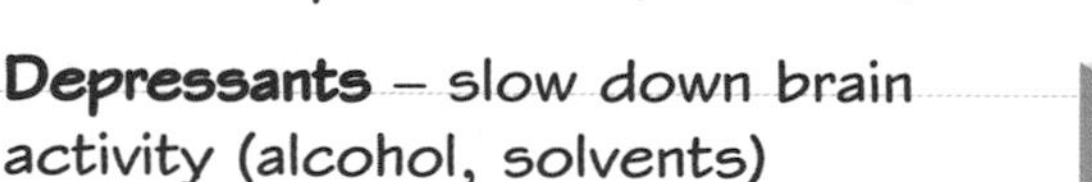

Depressants – slow down brain activity (alcohol, solvents)

Analgesics – painkilling drugs (aspirin, paracetamol, heroin)

UK alcohol laws

- Children under 16 are not allowed in a pub/bar unless with an adult.
- Under 18s are not allowed to drink alcohol in a pub/bar except if 16/17 and having a meal.
- Alcohol can be served 24 hours a day in licensed premises.
- It is illegal for anyone under 18 to buy alcohol.
- Everywhere that sells alcohol has to have a licence.
- It is illegal for anyone to try to buy alcohol for a child.

Now try this

1 Explain why the UK has drug and alcohol laws.
(c, 8 marks)

In Northern Ireland and Scotland there may be some differences to the laws above, so, if you live in either of these places, you may like to make clear where you come from and what the laws are.

Social and health problems caused by drugs and alcohol

There is much evidence of the social and health problems caused by the taking of drugs and drinking of alcohol.

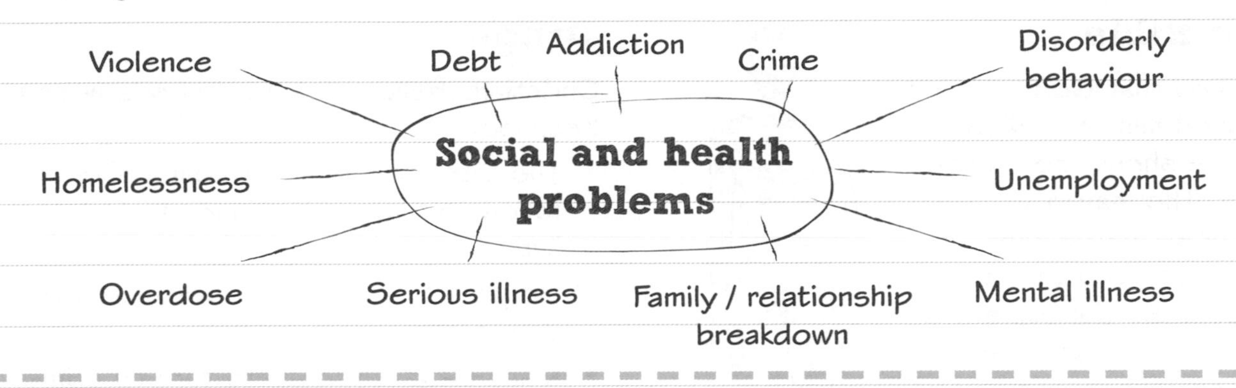

Alcohol

- Men should not drink more than 3–4 units a day.
- Women should not drink more than 2–3 units a day.
- Twice the recommended amount is classed as binge drinking.
- Health problems include heart disease, stroke, liver disease and cancer.
- Psychological and emotional breakdowns are also common effects.

An average pint of lager contains 2 units of alcohol.

Smoking

- Smoking leads to a range of health problems including cancer, lung disease and high blood pressure.
- Smokers have poor dental health and smell of nicotine and smoke.
- The addictive nature of smoking can interfere with romantic and social relationships.

Drugs

- Negative effects of illegal drugs include crime to fund addiction, unemployment and social disorder.
- Drugs can cause a possible loss of incentive to work and maintain a regular lifestyle.
- A serious overdose is a real danger.
- There are serious psychological effects of drug addiction, even after beating it.
- Drugs affect the brain and can lead to mental illness and loss of brain function.

Now try this

1 What is meant by **addiction**? **(a, 2 marks)**

2 Do you think drinking alcohol should be illegal? Give two reasons for your point of view. **(b, 4 marks)**

Make it clear that this is your own opinion. You could begin your answer with 'I think that…'.

Had a look ☐ Nearly there ☐ Nailed it! ☐

Christian attitudes to drugs and alcohol

Christians in the UK are completely **against** the taking of illegal drugs but have **differing** attitudes on alcohol.

The Bible

Teaches that God created human bodies and we should not abuse them. The majority of Christians believe taking any kind of drug excessively **damages** the body God created and is therefore wrong.

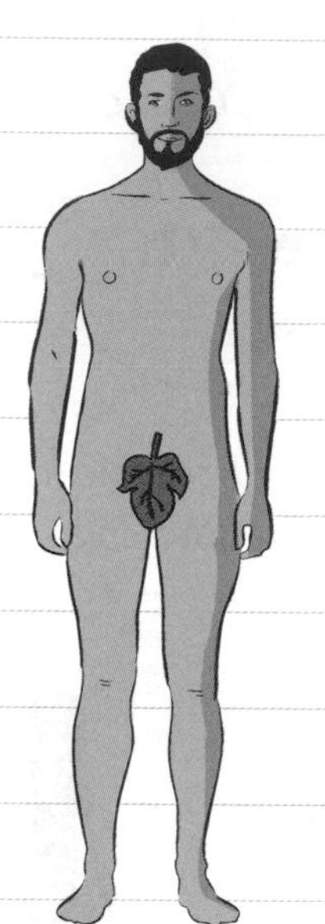

Drugs

Christians believe taking drugs is **wrong** because:

- The Bible teaches Christians should follow the law of the land in which they live.
- Illegal drugs are illegal because they are dangerous.
- Many illegal drug users turn to crime.
- Drug abuse leads to family breakups and makes people antisocial.
- Illegal drugs change a person's behaviour.

Reasons FOR drinking alcohol

✔ The Bible does not forbid alcohol.
✔ Jesus himself drank wine and performed a miracle of turning water into wine.
✔ Jesus gave his disciples wine at the Last Supper.
✔ St Paul told his friend Timothy to drink wine to help with digestion.

Many Churches today do not forbid alcohol and use it during Holy Communion.

Reasons for NOT drinking alcohol

✘ Drinking alcohol impairs a person's judgement and their ability to act in a Christian way.
✘ There are many other types of drink today.
✘ Alcohol today is much stronger than in the past.
✘ It is best to avoid offending others so do not drink at all.

Now try this

1 Explain why some Christians drink alcohol and some do not. **(c, 8 marks)**

2 'Christians should not drink alcohol'.
You should refer to at least one religion in your answer.
(i) Do you agree? Give reasons for your opinion. **(d, 3 marks)**
(ii) Give reasons why some people may not agree with you. **(3 marks)**

Take time to read the statement to make sure you understand the question. Explain each reason fully, possibly giving examples to help develop each reason.

Muslim attitudes to drugs and alcohol

Islam strongly **forbids** the use and sale of all alcohol and drugs. Here are some of the reasons Muslims believe alcohol and illegal drugs are wrong:

Muslim teachings

- All Muslims should avoid intoxicants because drugs and alcohol can affect a person and hinder their daily lives.
- Drugs and alcohol will have a negative effect on a person's relationships with others.
- Muhammad referred to alcohol as 'the mother of all sins'.

Putting it into practice

Muslims use stories and examples to show how drinking alcohol leads to bad decisions and further sin.

Many Muslims will not sell alcohol as part of their business nor work for a company that sells alcohol.

Now try this

1 Choose one religion other than Christianity and explain why some of its followers do not drink alcohol.

(c, 8 marks)

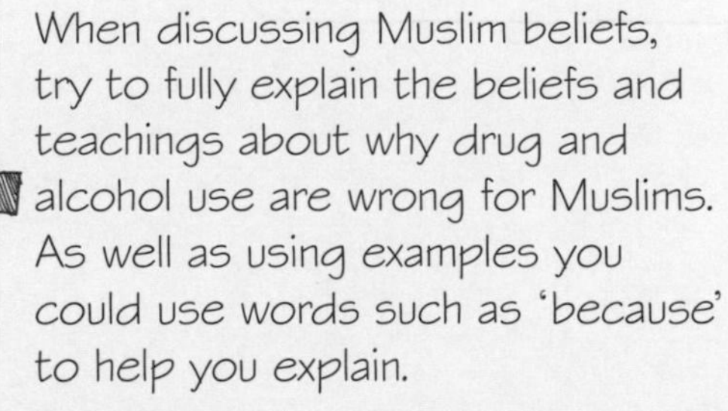

Had a look ☐ Nearly there ☐ Nailed it! ☐

Key words

It is important that you learn the key words for each topic. This is so you can explain what they mean for (a) type questions and use the key words in your answers to other questions to explain ideas fully.

Key words	Definitions
addiction	a recurring compulsion to engage in an activity regardless of its bad effects
capital punishment	the death penalty for a crime or offence
crime	an act against the law
deterrence	the idea that punishments should be of such a nature that they will put people off (deter) committing crimes
judgement	the act of judging people and their actions
justice	due allocation of reward and punishment / the maintenance of what is right
law	rules made by Parliament and enforceable by the courts
reform	the idea that punishments should try to change criminals so that they will not commit crimes again
rehabilitation	restore to normal life
responsibility	being responsible for one's actions
retribution	the idea that punishments should make criminals pay for what they have done wrong
sin	an act against the will of God

Exam skills: (a) questions and SPaG

Your exam paper is divided into four sections. Each section contains two full questions and you must choose one of these to answer in each section. You need to spend about 20 minutes answering each question. Each question has four parts, (a), (b), (c) and (d).

Spelling, punctuation and grammar

Before we look at (a) questions you need to know about some extra marks you can earn. In Section 1 of the Unit 8 exam paper, there are 4 marks available for spelling, punctuation and grammar. To be successful here, your spelling, punctuation and grammar need to be really good. Make sure that you use formal written English and not slang or text-speak, for example. You need to use these to help make what you want to say very clear. Also try to use a good range of key words accurately.

Example:

Its wot god would of wanted.

It is what God would have wanted. ✔

(a) type questions

(a) type questions are worth 2 marks and they ask you to **define a word**, for example:

What is meant by **responsibility**? **(2 marks)**

- You are asked to **give the meaning of one** of the key words.
- You might also be asked to give two examples of something.
- To do well you need to give a fully correct answer.

Worked example

What is meant by **deterrence**? **(2 marks)**

Sample answer

Deterrence is a word to do with punishment.

Improved sample answer

Deterrence is the idea that a punishment given to a criminal should be of such a nature that it will put other people off committing the same crime.

The first answer shows recognition of a link between deterrence and punishment but is not a full definition. The second answer is much better and is very similar to the glossary of key words.

Worked example

What is **The United Nations**? **(2 marks)**

The United Nations is an international organisation that was set up to promote world peace and cooperation between groups and nations.

The student has offered a good summary of the key phrase required so would achieve 2 marks.

Remember:

- Learn all your key words thoroughly.
- Keep your answers short and to the point but make sure you define the word or phrase clearly.
- You don't need to write more than one sentence as long as you explain the term fully.

Now try this

1 Write down your understanding of each of the following key words:
The Golden Rule **Pressure group** **Global warming** **Sin** **(a, 2 marks)**

Exam skills: (b) questions

(b) type questions are worth 4 marks and ask for **your opinion** on a point of view.

Applying your skills

To do well on a 4-mark question:

- Give **your own** opinion.
- Give **two reasons** to support your opinion.
- Try not to give brief reasons. Instead aim to offer **well-developed** reasons. Try to explain fully the reason you are giving.
- You can also give an example to support your reason, as a way of developing your answer.

Worked example

Do you agree with capital punishment? Give **two** reasons for your point of view. **(4 marks)**

Sample answer

I disagree with capital punishment because it makes you as bad as the criminal.

The first answer is very brief; it only offers one reason which is not well developed. The second answer is much improved offering two different reasons, each of which is well explained and developed.

Improved sample answer

I disagree with capital punishment because it makes society as bad as the criminal. It is against the law to kill so it should also be against the law to kill as a punishment. Secondly, killing a criminal can be seen as an easy way out. It would be better if the criminal had to spend a long time in jail to think about what they have done and suffer the guilt.

Remember:

- There are no right and wrong answers to these questions – just well reasoned answers.
- You **must** give your own **opinion** and **two reasons** why you think that.
- Make sure you offer two **different** reasons and use **examples** if possible to explain what you mean.
- Try to **develop** and **explain** your reasons.
- You can make reference to religious teachings you have studied but you do not have to as these questions focus on what **you** think.

Now try this

1 Do you think everyone should look after the environment? Give two reasons for your opinion. **(b, 4 marks)**

Try to apply the reasoning above to this question, building up your answer to achieve full marks.

Exam skills: (c) questions

(c) type questions are worth 8 marks. They ask you to **explain** a particular belief or idea.

Applying your skills

To do well on an 8-mark or (c) type question you must try to:

- **Explain** ideas fully – don't just make a list but explain why / how, use phrases such as 'this is because...'
- Use relevant and appropriate **examples** to support your explanation.
- Give **up to** four reasons to support your opinion.
- Start a **new paragraph** for each point. This makes it easier to check your answer at the end.
- The **fewer reasons** you give the **more well-developed** your answers need to be.

QWC

In the (c) questions you will also be assessed on your Quality of Written Communication (QWC). (You'll see a * next to the question.) You need to:

- Express your understanding clearly and using a good standard of English.
- Check your handwriting, spelling, punctuation and grammar.
- Use specialist vocabulary and religious key words.
- Plan and structure your answer carefully to suit the question.

Remember:

- Include a **variety** of reasons.
- Try **not** to just give brief reasons.
- Learn the content **thoroughly**.
- Learn some **key quotes** from the Bible or Qur'an to support what you say.
- There are marks available for **QWC**.

Worked example

Explain why some Christians agree with transplant surgery. **(8 marks)**

Most Christians will support transplant surgery because it saves lives. Jesus was a healer and we should be too.

Secondly, some Christians believe that they have an immortal soul and a new resurrection body, so they do not need their organs when they die. They would agree with donating organs as this would not affect their afterlife.

The Christian Church also teaches that Jesus advised Christians to 'Love they neighbour'. Donating an organ would reflect this idea and follow Jesus' Golden Rule.

Finally, the Parable of the Sheep and Goats teaches Christians that any good thing they do for someone is the same as helping Jesus. Some Christians will feel that becoming donating organs when they die is a good way to do this.

This answer has a set structure and each point is developed by offering a full explanation and examples.

The answer is clear and this is shown through the structured answer and use of specialist religious vocabulary.

Now try this

1 Explain Christian teachings and ideas about justice. **(c, 8 marks)**

Had a look ☐ Nearly there ☐ Nailed it! ☐

Exam skills: (d) questions

(d) type questions are worth 6 marks. They ask for **your opinion** and for you to also consider an **alternative** point of view.

Applying your skills

To do well on a 6-mark (d) question:

- Spend the **same** amount of **time** answering part (i) as you do answering part (ii).
- Offer **your opinion** and views on the statement.
- Show that you know why some people hold **different views** to you and why.
- **Refer to a religion** – you need to include at least one religious view.
- Give **evidence** or **examples** to support your points.

For each part of your answer:

A partial answer = 1 simple reason.

An improved answer = 2 simple reasons or 1 developed reason.

An even better answer = 3 simple reasons or 1 developed and 1 simple reason.

Worked example

'It does not matter if religious people drink alcohol.' In your answer you should refer to at least one religion.

i. Do you agree? Give reasons for your opinion. **(3 marks)**

I agree because drinking helps people relax and get along. Secondly, the Bible does not forbid the use of alcohol indeed wine is used in the celebration of Communion. Jesus himself turned water into wine at the wedding in Canaan.

ii. Give reasons why some people may disagree with you. **(3 marks)**

Muslims would disagree because the Qur'an forbids the drinking of alcohol. They believe alcohol keeps a Muslim from their duty to God as it should never be drunk. Some Christians also disagree because alcohol causes problems in society so Christians should not drink to set a good example.

The student has successfully shown both sides of the debate and made reference to at least one religion which is required by the question. Some of their points are more developed than others but they express themselves clearly and with good explanation.

Remember:

- Try to give up to **three** reasons.
- Have at least one **religious** view.
- Clearly **separate** the two parts of your answer.
- Give **reasons** to support your opinion. However, the **fewer** reasons you give the **more** well-developed your answers need to be.
- Think about the reasons you have learned about in class.

Now try this

1 'Religious believers should always oppose war.' In your answer you should refer to at least one religion.

(i) Do you agree? Give reasons for your opinion. **(d, 3 marks)**

(ii) Give reasons why some people may disagree with you. **(3 marks)**

Answers

Here we have given possible responses, however other approaches may also be suitable. The number given to each topic refers to its page number.

Believing in God

1. Introduction

1 Atheism is believing that God does not exist.
2 Omnipotence is the belief that God is all powerful.

2. Religious upbringing

1 • Christian parents teach their children to pray, praying to God will make children believe he exists.
- Christian parents take their children to church where they learn about their faith and about the existence of God, so will believe he does exist.
- Sunday school is where children hear about God existing and so will believe that he does.
- Many Christian parents send their children to a church school so they will learn about the existence of God.
- Christian parents encourage their children to be confirmed and make their own choices about belonging to the Christian faith.

2 Agree:
- Religion should be a free choice. Parents can guide their children but should not make decisions for them.
- Many children who are forced to follow a religion may rebel and turn away from it.
- It is better for a child to choose to follow a faith than be forced as their faith will be stronger.

Disagree:
- It is through parents raising their children within faith that children learn about it and are guided correctly.
- If parents don't bring their children up in faith, the religion may not be passed on and continue.
- Christian parents will want their children to be Christians because it is the only way they will get into heaven.
- It is part of a Muslims responsibility to Allah to bring up their children in the faith.

3. Religious experiences

1 A numinous experience is where a person believes they have experienced something greater than themselves, such as God. They may change as a result of this experience.
2 Agree:
- There is evidence of miracles in the world which could be God answering prayers.
- God may answer prayers through giving people the strength, comfort and support to cope with life – it may not be what they expect.

Disagree:
- God may listen to prayers but many people pray for things that aren't important, e.g. a new bike, so he wouldn't grant this.
- God cannot answer all prayers as this would mean changing events in the world.

4. The design argument

1 Agree:
- There is evidence of design in the world (e.g. the tides, planets) that suggests it could not have happened by chance and must have been planned.
- The universe is too complex to have happened without someone designing it that way.
- Paley's watch argument.

Disagree:
- Design comes from evolution which is a scientific theory and has nothing to do with God.
- There are faults with the world (e.g. earthquakes, tsunamis, famine). If it were designed, the designer would not have chosen to include these things.
- Evil and suffering show the world is not designed because more care would have been taken to not include these.

2 Agree:
- The Bible explains that God designed the world so Christians believe it was true.
- There is evidence of design in the world (e.g. the tides, planets) that suggests it could not have happened by chance and must have been planned.
- The universe is too perfect and complex to have happened without someone designing it that way. That person must have been very intelligent. Only God could have done this.
- Mention of Paley's watch argument.

Disagree:
- Design comes from evolution which is a scientific theory and has nothing to do with God.
- The world is not designed well, for example earthquakes, tsunamis etc. A God that is omnipotent and omni-benevolent would not have designed these.
- Evil and suffering show the world is not designed because a God that is all-loving would not have designed evil and suffering.

5. The causation argument

1 Agree:
- Anything as great as the universe needs a cause and God is the only possible cause.
- Something cannot come from nothing so the universe must have been caused by God.

Disagree:
- The Big Bang is the more likely cause of the universe.
- The universe may not need a cause.
- If God caused the universe, who caused God?

2 • If people hold this view, they are likely to strengthen their belief in God or have it confirmed.
- Causation argument states that the universe must have been caused by God as the universe could not have happened by chance, therefore leading to belief in God.
- Nothing causes itself so it must have been God that caused the universe.
- Reference to St Thomas Aquinas and the Cosmological Argument.

6. Scientific explanation of the origins of the world

1 Agree:
- Big Bang is a more popular explanation that makes sense, because it can be tested.
- Modern science has proven that the creation story in the Bible is wrong, and that God did not create the world.
- God is not needed to explain the existence of the Universe because there is evidence of the Big Bang and evolution.

Disagree:
- The world is too perfect and complex to have happened by chance so God must have created it.
- Reference to the design or causation arguments to argue that God created the world.

- Many Muslims and some Christians claim God caused the world using science, therefore meaning science and religion can work together to explain the existence of the universe.

7. Unanswered prayers

1 Prayer is an attempt to contact or communicate with God, usually through words.

2 Unanswered prayers can be a challenge to faith and belief in God:
- Some may turn away from God as they believe a loving God would answer their prayers.
- Many Christians may pray even more regularly to develop a deeper relationship with God and go on trusting him.
- Some may realise that he cannot answer all prayers because he has a wider plan for the world.
- Some prayers may not be answered because they are not too selfish. Give examples – e.g. for a car.

8. The problem of evil and suffering

1 Moral evil is actions performed by humans that cause suffering to others.

2
- If God is omnipotent, he has the power to remove evil and suffering.
- If God is omni-benevolent, he cares for his creation and doesn't want humans to suffer.
- If God is omniscient, he knows when humans suffer.
- If God existed, he would not allow evil and suffering to continue as he is meant to be omnipotent, omni-benevolent and omniscient.
- As evil and suffering do exist many people therefore argue that it proves God does not exist.

9. Christian responses to the problem of evil and suffering

1 Agree:
- There is so much evil and suffering and much of it seems pointless.
- Natural evil (not caused by humans) doesn't seem to have any reason.
- If God was all-loving and all-powerful he would remove evil and suffering. As evil and suffering exists, this must prove that God does not exist.

Disagree:
- Evil and suffering may have a purpose from God that humans do not understand.
- Just because there is evil and suffering in the world doesn't prove that God does not exist.

2 Agree:
- Evil and suffering may have a purpose humans don't know about, therefore they can explain it and still believe in God.
- Not all suffering is natural – much of it is moral that means humans are to blame. People have free will and make their own choices. This is not God's fault.
- The presence of evil and suffering doesn't mean that God doesn't exist. It may be a test from God to see how people will respond.
- Muslims believe evil and suffering is part of the test of life and therefore necessary.

Disagree:
- Evil and suffering challenges God's existence as a good and powerful God wouldn't allow humans to suffer.
- It challenges his existence as an omniscient God because if he were all-knowing, he would know how to remove evil and suffering.
- Many people feel that evil and suffering is the best evidence to be used to show God cannot exist.
- Either God is not omni-benevolent, omniscient and omnipotent or he does not exist.

10. The media and belief in God

1 Agree:
- Many programmes show religious ideas.
- People may see religious actions they haven't seen before and learn something new.
- They may gain new understanding and knowledge about religion.

Disagree:
- People aren't interested in religion today.
- The media offers news and entertainment not religion.
- Many shows on TV have no religion in them or show religion in a negative light.

2 Agree:
- Religious programme/films show religion positively, for example talking about their experiences of God or showing miracles.
- Examples of positive images of religion through the media.
- Many people have wrong ideas about religion so showing it on TV can correct these and have a positive impact on how they feel about belief in God.

Disagree:
- Many programmes about religion (e.g. the news) show religion negatively, for example religious tensions.
- Religion is often shown on TV to be strange and extreme, which does not give a positive image (e.g. documentaries on Scientology).
- Religion programmes can be boring and so give a negative image.

Matters of life and death

12. Christian beliefs in life after death

1 The idea that the soul lives on after the death of the body.

2 Agree:
- Death can't be the end – there must be something else.
- Religious teachings in the Bible (e.g. Jesus resurrection or example from Islam) prove that death is not the end.

Disagree:
- Why does there need to be something else? We could just die.
- There is no evidence of an afterlife.

13. The effect of belief in the afterlife on Christian lives

1
- Christians believe that there is an afterlife and that they will be judged after death. They will therefore live their lives trying to please God – living within the guidelines of the Bible and teachings of the Church.
- They will consider how they treat others.
- They are aware that their actions on earth will determine their afterlife and so will try to follow what their religion tells them to do.
- The promise of Heaven as a reward means this is what they will aim for.
- The evidence that Jesus rose gives them comfort and they won't be frightened of death.

14. Islamic beliefs about life after death

1 Islam:
- Belief in akhirah (life after death) is very important. The Qur'an says it is so.
- The Qur'an gives clear descriptions of Heaven and Hell.
- The Qur'an teaches that whether a person goes to Heaven or Hell is God's choice.
- The Qur'an and Shariah law teach that everything a Muslim does is judged by Allah and their actions will determine their afterlife.

2 Answers when choosing Islam:
- Muslims will try to perform good actions as they believe Allah is always watching them.
- They want to please Allah as they will be judged in the afterlife.
- They will try to perform good deeds.
- They will try to fulfil the Five Pillars in order to please Allah.
- They will try not to cause harm to others.

15. Non-religious belief in life after death

1 Agree:
- Mediums claim they can talk to dead people which is evidence of life after death.
- Protestant Christians believe that there is communication between the dead and the living and that the paranormal is evidence of this.
- Some people claim to remember ideas from past lives so must be living after death.

Disagree:
- Mediums have been proven to be fakes or cheats.
- Ghosts could be hallucinations.
- If there is reincarnation, wouldn't everyone remember ideas of a past life?

16. Non-belief in life after death

1
- There is no evidence of an afterlife.
- They believe mediums and other evidence of an afterlife is fake.
- They accept science rather than religious ideas.
- The body decays after death so they question how there can be any sort of afterlife.
- As a result, life after death seems impossible.

17. Abortion

1 Abortion is the removal of a foetus from the womb before it can survive.

2 Agree:
- Some people are not ready for children and should be given the choice.
- Women should have the right to make choices about their own body.

Disagree:
- Abortion can be seen as murder.
- Disabled children can often live full and happy lives.
- Embryos are potential humans and have a right to life.

18. Christian attitudes to abortion

1 Sanctity of life is the idea that life is holy and belongs to God.

2 Agree:
- It is sometimes the lesser of two evils.
- Jesus taught compassion towards others.
- We cannot be sure if life begins at conception.
- It should be available in cases of rape or incest.
- Medical technology allows us to see if there are problems with a foetus.
- Abortion may be the best choice in some circumstances, for example if the mother's life is at risk.

Disagree:
- Abortion can be viewed as murder.
- The Ten Commandments say that taking a life is wrong.
- Life begins at conception, abortion is therefore taking a life.
- Life is sacred and a gift from God, only God has the right to end a pregnancy.
- God has a plan for every human.
- All life has value, every person has a right to life, including a foetus.
- The Catholic Church teaches that abortion is always wrong.

19. Muslim attitudes to abortion

1 Agree:
- Abortion is viewed as murder which goes against the Ten Commandments.
- Life is sacred and a gift from God.
- God has a plan for every human.
- All life has value and life begins at conception.

Disagree:
- Jesus taught compassion towards others.
- We cannot be sure if life begins at conception.
- It should be available in some cases such as rape, incest, danger to the health of the mother or severe disability of the child.
- Medical technology allows us to see if there are problems with a foetus.
- In Islam, the soul enters the foetus at 120 days, so abortion could be allowed in some cases before this time.

20. Euthanasia

1 This is when a seriously ill person is assisted with what they need to commit suicide.

2 Agree:
- People have the right to choose what happens to them in their life.
- No-one should suffer a painful death.
- There is no point in being kept alive if there is no quality of life.
- The patient can die with dignity.

Disagree:
- Life is special and scared even for people who are not religious.
- Euthanasia is murder and murder is wrong.
- Some people may be pressured into choosing euthanasia by their family.
- Hospices and palliative care means there is no need for euthanasia.

21. Christian attitudes to euthanasia

1 Agree:
- Quality of life is important.
- It may be the lesser of two evils.
- Jesus taught Christians to 'Love thy neighbour' and a gentle death may be the most loving thing.

Do not agree:
- It is taking away a person's life, which is murder. The Bible says that people must not commit murder (Ten Commandments).
- God created humans in his image so only he has the power to take away life.
- Life is sacred and should be valued.
- There are alternatives such as hospices so it is not necessary.
- God has a plan for every human and it is not for us to intervene. A person on life support is already dead so you are keeping them alive and interfering with Gods plan.

22. Muslim attitudes to euthanasia

1 Answers when choosing Islam:
- The Qur'an says that suicide is wrong and so assisted suicide and voluntary euthanasia are wrong.
- Muslims believe in the sanctity of life and so non-voluntary euthanasia would be murder which is banned by the Qur'an.
- The Qur'an says that only Allah has the right to give and take life, so euthanasia would be a sin (disobeying Allah).
- Muslims regard life as a test and ending life early would be like cheating in the test and would lead to hell on the Last Day.
- The Shari'ah bans euthanasia.

2 Agree:
- The Shari'ah bans euthanasia so Muslims should oppose euthanasia.
- Only Allah or God have the right to take life.
- The Ten Commandments say that murder is wrong, so Christians should also oppose assisted suicide and euthanasia as these end life.

Disagree:
- It may be the lesser of two evils.
- Jesus taught Christians to 'Love thy neighbour' and a gentle death may be the most loving thing.
- Some Muslims allow terminal patients to choose not to continue with medical treatment if it is causing hardship or family distress.

23. Matters of life and death in the media

1 Agree:
- It is important these issues are shown and discussed in the media.
- There are strong opinions on these issues so they should be discussed.
- Religious views may be out of date today.

Disagree:
- It is wrong to present only one view on an issue.
- Religious views should be respected as they have been around for a long time and lots of people believe in them.

Marriage and the family

25. Changing attitudes towards marriage, divorce, family and homosexuality in the UK

1 Cohabitation is when a couple live together but are not married.

2 Homosexuality is when someone is sexually attracted to someone of the same sex.

3 Agree:
- People are more tolerant today of differences.
- The Church and teachings have less influence today.
- There are fewer religious ceremonies and more people choosing to cohabit.

Disagree:
- Marriage is still important today and people still get married.
- People are choosing to have different types of ceremonies not just religious ones, rather than not getting married.

26. Christian attitudes to sex outside marriage

1 Promiscuity is having sex with a number of different partners without commitment.

2
- Christianity teaches that sex outside marriage is wrong.
- Sex should only take place within marriage as it is an act of love and commitment.
- Christians are taught to avoid casual relationships.
- The Bible only allows sex between marriage partners, for example the Ten Commandments teaches that adultery is wrong.
- Children born outside of marriage may not have a stable upbringing.
- Sex helps to unite a couple and should take place within marriage.

27. Muslim attitudes to sex outside marriage

1 Most Muslims are against sex outside marriage because:
- Sex before marriage is forbidden by the Qur'an.
- The Shari'ah says that sex should only take place in marriage.
- Children should only be born in a family where the mother and father are married.
- Adultery is condemned by Allah in the Qur'an.
- Adultery is likely to harm the family which the Qur'an and Shari'ah regard as very important.

28. Christian attitudes to divorce

1 Agree:
- Some circumstances require it – e.g. abuse or adultery.
- Sometimes couples fall out of love.
- Christians believe it is better to divorce than live in hatred and quarrel all the time.

Disagree:
- Marriage vows state that marriage is intended to be for life.
- It is a commitment made before God.
- Jesus taught that divorce is wrong, in Marks's Gospel.

29. Muslim attitudes to divorce

1 Islam

Accept:
- Marriage is a contract in Islam not a promise to Allah.
- The Qur'an allows it.
- There are rules for how divorce must happen.
- It may be better for children to live with divorced parents than arguing.

Do not accept:
- Muhammad disliked divorce.
- Muhammad said divorce was the most hated thing.
- Divorce damages the lives of children.
- Divorce is disrespectful to the family.

30. Christian teachings on family life

1 Agree:
- Family is where children are taught.
- A supportive family is best.
- Everyone needs someone to care for them.

Disagree:
- Some families are not supportive.
- Sometimes family members can abuse their relationships.
- Some people are better off on their own.

2 Agree:
- Children can be taught and brought up correctly.
- Children are given a stable and safe upbringing.
- This is what God intended. The Bible teaches that God commanded humans to 'be fruitful and multiply' (Genesis 1:28).
- God intended children to be created between a married couple because the Bible teaches that sex should only happen within marriage.

Disagree:
- Many people today cohabit which is another form of commitment where children can be raised.
- A couple don't have to be married to bring their children up in a loving environment.
- Two parents who love each other will provide the best environment for children.

31. Muslim teachings on family life

1 Agree:
- Less people are choosing to marry and raise children.
- Society today is different.
- Many people choose to cohabit rather than marry.

Disagree:
- Family is important as it is where children are raised and taught the difference between wrong and right.
- In Islam, family is the heart of the community and is where many religious activities take place.
- In Islam, Muslim values are taught within the family, which shows the importance of the family.
- Families still care and support each other.

32. Christian attitudes to homosexuality

1 A civil partnership is a legal ceremony which gives a homosexual couple the same rights as husband and wife.
2 Do allow:
- Some Christians believe it is perfectly natural and all humans were created equal by God.
- Some Christians will bless a civil partnership.
- Same sex couples should be allowed to express their commitment to another person.
- Jesus taught to 'love thy neighbour' and this includes all people.

Don't allow:
- Marriage was intended by God to be one man and one woman.
- Same sex partners cannot have children naturally which is a purpose of marriage.
- Homosexuality undermines the family.
- The Bibles teaches it is wrong.

33. Muslim attitudes to homosexuality

1 Islam:
- Homosexuality is banned in the Qur'an.
- It is punishable by death according to Shari'ah law.
- It is believed to be harmful to the health of individuals.
- Seen as a threat to the stability of Islam.

34. Christian attitudes to contraception

1 Contraception is intentionally preventing pregnancy from occurring.
2 Agree:
- It allows family planning so there are not too many people born.
- Contraception is sensible to stop unwanted pregnancies and the spread of disease.

Disagree:
- People should just go out and have a good time.
- Some Christians condemn all forms of artificial contraception so feel it is right not to use contraception.
- You can't use contraception if you want a child.

35. Muslim attitudes to contraception

1 Islam – Muslims are divided on their views about contraception.

Agree:
- It allows family planning so there are not too many people born.
- Contraception is sensible to stop unwanted pregnancies and the spread of disease.
- It can improve women's health.
- We should have the right to choose.

Disagree:
- In religion, the purpose of sex is to have children, so contraception would prevent this.
- Some contraceptives cause early abortions.
- It is important for religious people to have children to continue the faith.

2 Islam:

Accept:
- Life of the mother should be preserved.
- Muhammad supported natural methods (e.g. the withdrawal method).
- Contraception is sometimes taught to be acceptable for economic reasons (e.g. to prevent large families where income is low).
- Married couples can choose to use it for sensible family planning.

Do not accept:
- Having children is an important duty in Islam and contraception would prevent this.
- In strict Islamic countries, only natural methods are allowed.
- Life is sacred and a gift from God, so Muslims should not prevent this.

Religion and community cohesion

37. Changing attitudes to gender roles in the UK

1 Sexism is discrimination against people because of their gender (being male or female).
2
- Traditional view of women in society was to stay at home and look after the children.
- Traditional view of men in society was to go out to work and earn.
- There is more equality today with women being given the vote and being better educated.
- Men are more involved with the childcare and home-life.
- These roles have changed because of the law and the way in society has developed.

38. Christian attitudes to equal rights for women

1 Agree:
- Jesus treated men and women the same.
- All humans were created equal by God.
- Women have equal rights in UK society.
- Church of England has female clergy.

Disagree:
- Men and women are different and may be suited to different roles.
- Catholic Church only allows male priests.
- Traditionally, men and women have not been given the same rights within religion.

39. Muslim attitudes to equal rights for women

1 Agree:
- Many Christians allow women to be priests.
- Many Christians believe that the Church should keep up with society.
- The Bible says they are equal.
- In Islam men and women have different but equal roles.

Disagree:
- Women are not allowed to be priests in Catholicism.
- Women cannot be Bishops.
- In Islam, women are not in positions of authority within Mosques.

40. The UK as a multi-ethnic society

1 An ethnic minority is a member of an ethnic group that is smaller than the majority.
2 Racism is the belief that some races are superior and therefore more important than others.

41. Government action to promote community cohesion

1 Community cohesion is when there is a common vision and shared sense of belonging for all groups in society.
2 Answer may refer to:
- Race Relations Act 1976.
- Commission for Racial Equality.
- Illegal to use abusive or insulting words of a racial nature.
- 'Britishness test' introduced to ensure common vision and sense of belonging.
- Organisations set up to ensure people from ethnic minorities are supported.

42. Why Christians should promote racial harmony

1 Agree:
- Teachings of Jesus – Christians want to follow his examples (give examples such as the Good Samaritan).
- Golden Rule 'Treat others as you would like to be treated'.
- Christians should put this into practice and treat everyone the same.
- Christians will be judged by God.

Disagree:
- It is not just up to Christians – everyone should have a responsibility to help.
- To be successful everyone has a role to play.

2 Agree:
- They follow their teachings and try to stop racism.
- Examples of people like Martin Luther King, Desmond Tutu, Church of England Race and Community Relationships committee.

Disagree:
- There is always more that can be done.
- It is everyone's responsibility to help stop racism.
- There is evidence of religious people acting in a racist way, for example the Ku Klux Klan.

43. Why Muslims should promote racial harmony

1 Islam:
- There are Muslims of every race.
- The concept of the Ummah means that all Muslims are brothers regardless of race.
- The Qur'an teaches that Allah made all the races on earth and so Islam teaches that people should give each other equal respect.
- Muhammad chose an African as his first prayer caller showing that he believed all races should be treated equally and Muslims should follow the example of the Prophet.
- Muhammad said in his last sermon that no race is superior to any other.
- Muhammad told Muslims that they are one community who should treat each other as brothers which means promoting racial harmony.

44. The UK as a multi-faith society

1 A multi-faith society is where many different religious groups live together in one society.

2
- A greater sense of tolerance and understanding.
- Varied and rich cultural life.
- New ways of living and enjoying life.
- Better understanding of different cultures and viewpoints increases understanding of others and broadens horizons.

45. Issues raised about multi-faith societies

1 This is a marriage where the husband and wife are from different religions.

2 Agree:
- Christians should try and help others achieve salvation.
- In some religions, it is taught as a duty (e.g. Mormons).
- Some people believe their religion is the only correct one so they should show followers of other religions the correct way.
- It is part of the right to religious freedom.

Disagree:
- It could be seen as prejudice when living in a multi-faith society, by discriminating against those of a different religion.
- No one should try to force anyone to believe anything.
- Faith is a personal matter.

46. Religion and community cohesion

1 Agree:
- Many religions teach that they should promote community cohesion.
- They have set up groups that can be used to do more, such as the Interfaith Network.
- Christianity teaches that everyone is equal, for example the Golden Rule, so Christians should work to promote this.
- Islam also teaches that everyone is equal.

Disagree:
- It is the responsibility of every person not just religious believers.
- The government can bring about real changes.
- There are many religious groups already established to promote community cohesion such as the Interfaith Network and the Muslim Council of Britain.

2 Agree:
- If people from different religions are seen to be working together, it sends out the right message.
- Many religions have common ideas.
- There are examples of groups that do this such as the Interfaith Network.

Disagree:
- Many ideas in different religions are too different.
- They is very little agreement.

47. Religion and community cohesion in the media

1 To answer this question you need to give one specified issue and refer to at least one type of media:
- Storylines on TV can be used to highlight ideas concerning a particular issue.
- The news can present the issue in positive ways, give examples.
- Journalists can report on ways in which religions are working together.
- Give examples that show how the media presents the chosen issue such as films, television, radio etc.

2 Agree:
- Often they present a negative view of certain religions to sell more or make the programme seem more interesting, give example.
- The negative aspects of religion are more entertaining than the positive.

Disagree:
- Newspapers report on events so it is accurate rather than biased.
- Often stories are positive rather than negative, give an example.

50. Unit 1 Exam skills (b) questions

1 Agree:
- Men and women have the same rights e.g. voting and the right to equal pay.
- Men and women can do the same jobs.
- Men take a more active role in the home.

Disagree:
- Women cannot be Catholic priests showing they are not equal.
- Men and women are traditionally seen to have different roles in society.
- Inequalities still exist – there are fewer women in positions of power.

51. Unit 1 Exam skills (c) questions

1
- Some believe evil and suffering is a test from God.
- Some believe humans have been given freewill by God and are responsible as many types of evil are caused by humans.

- Some may accept that evil has a purpose and happens for a reason because God has a plan for us all.
- Many Christians may pray more regularly. They may ask God for the strength to cope or pray for others, or strengthen their faith.
- Volunteering for a charity or organisation that supports others in need.
- They may attend church more often and try to follow the example if Jesus more in their lives.

52. Unit 1 Exam skills (d) questions

1 Agree:
- There are too many differences and conflicts as a result.
- There is not enough understanding between religions.
- Beliefs and ideas may conflict and lead to tensions (examples of tensions e.g. Bradford Riots).

Disagree:
- This will help different religions to understand each other and show characteristics of tolerance and respect.
- The Bible teaches the Golden Rule of treating others as you would like to be treated which means that we should treat each other equally and be able to live peacefully.
- The Qur'an teaches that no race is better than any other.

Rights and responsibilities

53. Christians and the Bible

1 The Bible is the Christian holy book which contains the words of God.

2
- Believed to be the word of God and Christians want to live as God intended as they believe he will judge them.
- Contains advice and guidance to help Christians in their lives.
- Contains the laws and rules of God such as the Ten Commandments.
- New Testament offers moral guidance and teachings on how Christians should behave (e.g. St Peter and St Paul).
- Contains the teachings of Jesus whose example they should follow.

54. Christians and the authority of the Church

1 Agree:
- Ideas can be discussed with Church members and help or advice given.
- God speaks to Christians through the Church.
- The Church can consider and explain Christian teachings in order to offer guidance.

Disagree:
- There are better sources of authority such as the Bible or conscience.
- Members of the Church may offer different advice which could be confusing.
- It only offers one point of view (that of the Bible) which may not be right.

2
- God speaks to Christians through the Church, so following the word of the Church, is the same as following the word of God.
- The Church is the body of Christ meaning it continues to be Jesus acting within the world.
- Leaders of the Church have had training and education so are best suited to offer guidance.
- The Church's teachings are important as they offer guidance and rules of what to do in certain situations.

55. Christians and the conscience

1 The conscience is a person's inner voice or an inner feeling of the rightness or wrongness of an action.

2 Agree:
- There are better sources of authority such as the Bible.
- A person's conscience may be wrong.
- What one person thinks is right may not be what the majority feel is right.
- Many Christians feel they should also consult the Bible and the Church to receive the best guidance.

Disagree:
- A person should rely on their own ideas and thoughts.
- A person always knows when something is right or wrong.
- Some Christians believe the conscience is God's voice telling them what to do and guiding them, therefore it is reliable.

56. Christians and Situation Ethics

1 Social change is the way in which society has changed and is changing.

2
- Love is the main principle and is also connected to the Golden Rule of 'Treat others as you would like to be treated'.
- Christians should follow the rules of the Bible.
- Most people would like to be treated in the most loving way.
- Example of Jesus seeming to follow Situation Ethics (acted in the most loving way towards woman accused of adultery).
- Every situation is judged individually and has a genuine Christian intention.

57. Christians and the variety of moral authorities

1 Agree:
- Moral decisions are not straightforward and using a variety of sources will provide more advice.
- Different sources of authority will strengthen each other.
- Some Christians believe the Bible was written a long time ago and should be used alongside other sources.

Disagree:
- Some forms of authority may be wrong.
- How do you know which is right if they contradict each other?
- Some Christians feel the Bible is true and contains the word of God. There is no need for another source.

58. Human rights in the UK

1 Human rights are the rights and freedoms to which everyone is entitled.

2 Agree:
- All humans are equal.
- God intended for all people to be treated the same (Golden Rule).

Disagree:
- Some people do not deserve to be treated the same (e.g. criminals).
- Some people need to be treated differently to meet their needs (e.g. disabled people).

59. Why human rights are important to Christians

1
- All Christians support the Universal Declaration of Human Rights.
- Every human was created by God in God's image and all of God's creations should be treated with respect.
- God loves everyone equally so they should be treated the same.
- The teachings of the Bible are in line with human rights teachings (e.g. Golden Rule, Love thy neighbour, the Parable of the Sheep and the Goats).

2 Agree:
- Every human was created by God and in God's image. All of God's creations should be treated equally and with respect.
- The teachings of the Bible are in line with human rights teachings (examples e.g. Golden Rule, Love thy neighbour).
- Christians believe God is a just God so his laws must be the best way to ensure human rights.

Disagree:
- Sometimes the law or religious ideas could be wrong.
- Sometimes the law needs to be fair to everyone and religion may not be.
- Not everyone follows the same religion and so this may exclude some people.
- Society has changed and religious rules do not always reflect this.

60. The importance of democratic and electoral processes

1 Electoral processes are the ways in which voting is organised.
2 Agree:
- They may have valid opinions.
- They need to be represented.
- The decisions made by those elected affect those under 18 too.

Disagree:
- They are too young to understand the significance.
- They may not be able to offer an objective or well-informed opinion.

61. Christian teachings on moral duties and responsibilities

1 Agree:
- Treating others as you would like to be treated makes sense and is always valid.
- Most people would want to be treated this way.
- It gives the same message as Human Rights, which are very relevant.

Disagree:
- This may not be appropriate in some situations.
- Some people deserve to be treated differently – either better or worse, for example those with disabilities may have different needs.

62. The nature of genetic engineering

1 Genetic engineering is the process where the structures and characteristics of genes are changed.
2 Agree:
- It helps us understand humans and animals better (genetic disorders).
- It helps to save lives through the knowledge it provides (crops resistant to disease or harsh climates, gene therapy).

Disagree:
- We do not yet know the long term effects of it.
- In the wrong hands, it could be misused.
- Sanctity of life – God created life and it should not be interfered with.

63. Christian attitudes to genetic engineering

1 Agree:
- Sanctity of Life – life is special and a gift from God and humans should not take on this role.
- Some Christians believe removing embryos is wrong as they are later destroyed. They believe life is created at conception and so this is murder, which is against the Ten Commandments.
- Genetic engineering should not be used to correct 'defects', God has a plan for everyone.

Disagree:
- God has given humans dominion and stewardship over the world and this technology is acceptable if used correctly.
- The Golden Rule teaches us to treat others as we would want to be treated so genetic engineering being used to save life, or improve life is acceptable.
- Jesus healed many people which suggests we should preserve life.

Environmental and medical issues

65. Global warming

1 Global warming is the increase in the temperature of the Earth's atmosphere (thought to be caused by the greenhouse effect).
2 Agree:
- Climate change seems to suggest we have an issue.
- The environment seems to be suffering e.g. extreme weather, drought, famine, melting of polar ice caps. This will have an effect on wildlife, plants and humans.

Disagree:
- There are other bigger problems in the world.
- Problems to do with people are more important and concerning than nature.

66. Pollution

1 Agree:
- We have to live on Earth so should help not harm it.
- We should preserve the Earth for future generations.
- God has given Humans have been given dominion and stewardship of the Earth.

Disagree:
- We should be more concerned with problems facing humans, such as war and disease than the environment.
- Many of us recycle which is enough.

2
- Burning of fossil fuels releases chemicals into the atmosphere.
- Driving vehicles on the roads releases chemicals.
- Overusing the world's natural resources (burning coal pollutes the atmosphere and oil spills endanger animal and plant life).
- Factories and air pollution.
- Noise and sight pollution.
- Problems of waste and dumping in landfill sites.

67. Natural resources

1 Natural resources are naturally occurring materials such as oil and fertile land which are used by humans.
2 Agree:
- If we continue to use them there will be none left.
- We have alternative renewable sources of energy (examples wind, solar).
- We should try to save and preserve the environment because Christians believe it is God's creation and he gave humans stewardship of the Earth.

Disagree:
- Why should we think of the future – we should make the most of life now.
- It is more expensive and harder to use renewable sources of energy.
- Not all renewable sources of energy are possible in certain places so we have to use what we have.

68. Christian teachings on stewardship and attitudes to the environment

1 Creation is the act of creating the universe or the universe which has been created.

2
- Stewardship – Christians believe they have a responsibility from God to care for the world for future generations.

- God created the world so Christians believe they should care for it.
- Dominion – Christians believe they have a position of power over the world and responsibility to care for it.
- Responsibility – Christians believe they are responsible for the world.
- Jesus taught Christians to love and help each other so humans should share the resources of the world more equally.

69. Muslim teachings on stewardship and attitudes to the environment

1 Agree:
- Everyone lives on the Earth so should help to care for it.
- All humans should preserve the Earth for future generations.
- Muslims believe that Allah created the world and that they have a responsibility to care for it as khalifahs (caretakers).

Disagree:
- The Earth is here to enjoy rather than work on.
- There is more to life than caring for the world.
- We should care for people as well as the Earth.

70. Medical treatment for infertility

1 Infertility is not being able to have children.

2 Agree:
- Money could be put to better use e.g. helping to find a cure for cancer.
- There are alternative ways of having a child e.g. adoption.
- Money could be used to help people who are alive rather than potentially creating a person.

Disagree:
- Everyone deserves the right to a child.
- Christianity teaches that God commanded humans to 'be fruitful and multiply' so fertility treatment helps some people try to achieve God's wishes.
- Having a family is what God intended people to do.
- Some people will go to any lengths to have a child and would say it was worth it.

71. Christian attitudes to fertility treatments

1 Support:
- God has given humans the ability to have children this way.
- It allows couples to experience the joy of a child.
- It follows teachings such as 'love your neighbour' and the Golden Rule.
- Christianity teaches that God commanded humans to 'be fruitful and multiply' (Genesis 1:28).

Don't support:
- God intended children to be created naturally through the act of sex between a husband and wife.
- No one has a 'right' to have a child.
- Masturbation is a sin and fertility treatments require this to get the sperm from the man.
- Some Christians believe life begins at conception. In treatments unused embryos may be destroyed and this can be seen as murder, which goes against the Ten Commandments.
- Surrogacy or egg/sperm donation could be seen as adultery, which also goes against the Ten Commandments.

2 Agree:
- Everyone should have the right to have a child if they wish.
- Having a family is what God intended and this fulfils that wish. Christianity teaches that God commanded humans to 'be fruitful and multiply' (Genesis 1:28).
- Infertility is not their fault.
- Providing fertility treatment free of charge follows the Golden Rule of treating others as you would want to be treated.

Disagree:
- It would cost too much money.
- No one has a 'right' to have a child.
- God has a plan for everyone and we should respect this.
- The money could be put to a different and perhaps better use.

72. Muslim attitudes to fertility treatments

1 Islam

Agree:
- Infertility is considered a disease so it is okay to try and find a cure.
- Having children is very important. The role and status of the woman in Muslim society involves her ability to have children.
- Having children unites a couple and keeps them together.
- Sperm and egg of the married couple are often used which is acceptable.
- God has given people the ability to create life this way.

Disagree:
- Some accept that if Allah does not want a couple to have a child they should accept it.
- Muslims disagree with the use of surrogacy and donor eggs or donor sperm as these are considered to be adultery.

73. Transplant surgery

1 Agree:
- This would encourage more people to donate.
- The money could go to help their family after their death.

Disagree:
- Is it morally acceptable? Will people be kept alive or allowed to die purely for organ donation?
- There could be issues with people 'selling' organs and this could be dangerous, exploiting those in financial need.
- You shouldn't be paid for things that are no use to you any longer.

2
- It allows the use of organs that otherwise might be wasted.
- It gives people an opportunity to help others after their death.
- The Golden Rule teaches that we should treat others as we should want to be treated and in donating organs for transplant or carrying out transplant surgery, we are doing this.
- It helps to save lives.
- It offers hope to the families of others and comfort to the family of the deceased.
- Most organs come from donors who have died who don't need them.

74. Christian attitudes to transplant surgery

1 Organ donation is giving organs to be used in transplant surgery.

2 Agree:
- It is a loving and charitable act which follows the teachings of Jesus about helping each other (the Golden Rule).
- It raises no problems for life after death as the body is not needed.

Disagree:
- It goes against the sanctity of life argument that life is special.
- It interferes with God's plans for every individual.
- Some Christians believe that the body and soul will be reunited, so the body would need to be intact.

75. Muslim attitudes to transplant surgery

1 Agree:
- It is up to the individual and no one should be forced.
- Organ donation is a big decision and should only be made by the individual or their next of kin.
- Organ donation should be voluntary and there could be ethical problems if the decision was influenced from any outside sources.
- Muslims believe that it goes against the sanctity of life that only God can give and take away.
- Muslims also believe that the body will be resurrected, so Islam cannot advise on this.

Disagree:
- Religious beliefs are important to followers and offer them guidance on what is right and wrong.
- It may be right or wrong to perform certain actions according to religion.
- Some Christians feel that organ donation is a positive action and are encouraged to be donors.
- Organ donation is a loving and charitable act which follows the teaching of Jesus to love one another (the Golden Rule, Love thy neighbour), therefore believers should follow this advice.
- It helps to decide in what circumstances it should be allowed, for example Muslims may support live donation and organ donation to help save the life of another.

2 Islam

Disagree:
- The Qur'an teaches that the body should not be interfered with after death and buried straight away.
- Muslims believe the body will be resurrected on the last day and therefore the organs will be needed.
- It goes against the sanctity of life argument that all life is sacred and special.

Agree:
- However, The Muslim Law Council supports it as it is a means of saving life.
- Some argue that it is ok if done to save the life of others as this is what Allah would wish.
- Live donations may be more acceptable as the resurrection of the body would be unaffected.

Peace and conflict

77. Why do wars occur?

1
- Self defence.
- Economics or natural resources.
- Fear.
- National pride.
- Fighting against aggression.
- Racial or ethnic hatred.
- Protecting people.
- Examples of the above from a suitable conflict e.g. Darfur, Afghanistan, Arab Spring among others.

78. The United Nations and world peace

1 The United Nations is an international body set up to promote world peace and co-operation.

2 Explain how the United Nations work for world peace using a relevant example:
- Arms control and disarmament.
- Conflict resolution and reconciliation.
- Organise peace talks.
- Restrict trade until countries begin to discuss issues.
- Send in peacekeeping forces to achieve peace.
- Relevant examples to support the above, e.g. Arab Spring, Darfur.

79. Religious organisations and peace

1 Forgiveness is when someone is no longer blamed for something and they are pardoned for what they did wrong.

2 Agree:
- It is only through action that peace will be achieved.
- Organisations are well placed to try and bring resolution and people together.
- Jesus taught Christians to 'Love thy neighbour' and encouraging world peace is part of this.

Disagree:
- They work so hard anyway to try and achieve peace.
- Many of their actions already result in success.
- Governments need to do more for World Peace.

80. Just war theory

1 Just war theory is a war that is fought for the right reasons and in the right way.

2
- Just war theory was developed by St Thomas Aquinas to help religious believers decide whether war is right (or just).
- It is fought with the aim of bringing peace.
- It is usually a last resort after all other options have been tried.
- Loss of life should be minimal rather than the aim of war.
- The methods used are fair and reasonable.

81. Christian attitudes to war

1 Will fight:
- Just war theory has been accepted by many Churches.
- There is teaching in the Bible that support just war theory: Jesus told the people they should obey the law and government of the country; St Paul told the people that they should obey people in authority.
- Violence may sometimes be necessary in order to achieve peace (e.g. in the case of invasion).
- There are situations where war is the lesser of two evils.

Will not fight:
- Believe in pacifism and war solves nothing.
- Do not agree with violence of any kind, Ten Commandments forbids killing.
- Believes the Bible has a message of peace, reconciliation and forgiveness, Jesus taught that people should love their enemies, Jesus stopped his own followers from using violence.

82. Muslim attitudes to war

1 Agree:
- If people need protecting then it is acceptable.
- When life is at risk or threatened then it is.
- If fought for a just cause (e.g. to defend Islam).
- If it is authorised by a Muslim authority.

Disagree:
- Innocent people are always killed.
- War never really achieves peace.

2 Some Muslims may accept war in exceptional circumstances because:
- Lesser jihad means holy war. Muslims recognise that sometimes it is necessary to fight in war as a last resort.
- The Qur'an teaches that Muslims should fight if they are attacked.
- Muhammad fought in many wars so by doing so Muslims are following his example.
- The Qur'an teaches that anyone who fights in a just war goes straight to Heaven therefore showing it has some purpose.
- The minimum amount of suffering should be caused and civilians should not be attacked.

However, some Muslims feel that:
- Peace is at the heart of Islam.

- Modern warfare means innocent people will always be killed which goes against Islamic principles.
- Non-violent methods are the only way to achieve peace.
- Violence only leads to more violence.

83. Christian attitudes to bullying

1 Agree:
- Usually bullies are suffering themselves and need help.
- Bullies are only picking on others because they are weaker.
- Perhaps bullies need educating in order to understand that what they are doing is wrong.
- Jesus taught that Christians should 'Love thy neighbour' therefore bullies should be helped rather than punished, otherwise you are as bad as the bully.

Disagree:
- Bullies must be stopped if we are going to move on.
- There is no excuse for picking on another person. Jesus taught that people should love one another and follow the Golden Rule.

84. Muslim attitudes to bullying

1 Agree:
- There is always more that can be done.
- School is a good place to educate bullies that what they are doing is wrong.
- Islam teaches that Muslims should work together to challenge wrongdoing.

Disagree:
- Bullying is part of life and makes a person tougher.
- We should be tackling bullying in other places too.

2 Islam
- The Qur'an teaches that all Muslims should work together to challenge any wrongdoing that causes harm.
- Islam teaches aggression or violence without just cause is wrong.
- Every person was created by Allah and it is wrong to abuse any part of his creation.
- Islam teaches Muslims should work to end injustice and cruelty.
- Muhammad taught that Muslims should protect and help the weak and vulnerable.
- All Muslims believe that on the last day they will be judged by Allah on the way they lived their lives.

85. Religious conflicts within families

1 Agree:
- There is added pressure to follow a religion.
- It may be difficult for religious parents to accept that their child does not want to be religious.
- Religious values may conflict with those of a child's peers.

Disagree:
- All families have conflict – it is part of being a family.
- Different types of conflict affect people in different ways.

2
- A child may want to convert to another faith or be an atheist.
- A child of atheist parents may become religious which is difficult to accept because of differences in opinion.
- There may be different ideas and expectations about social behaviour, moral issues and jobs and careers.
- Religious parents may not approve of their child's boyfriend/girlfriend.
- They may hold different ideas about how children should be raised.

86. Christian teachings on forgiveness and reconciliation

1 Agree:
- It's difficult but always possible if you try.
- By following the example of Jesus – Jesus died on the cross to bring forgiveness and reconciliation between humanity and God.

Disagree:
- Some actions are unforgiveable, such as murder.
- It is difficult sometimes to forget what a person has done.

2 Agree:
- They should try to follow the example of Jesus who died on the cross to bring forgiveness and reconciliation between humanity and God.
- The Bible teaches that forgiveness is important, '… if you hold anything against anyone, forgive him …' (Mark 11:25).
- Christians should forgive others and God will help them to do this even when it is difficult.
- It helps them to move on with their lives.

Disagree:
- Some actions are unforgiveable, such as murder.
- It is hard to follow their religion when they feel strongly about something.
- If it goes against a teaching in the Bible, Christians believe they do not have to forgive.

87. Muslim teachings on forgiveness and reconciliation

1 Forgiveness means to stop blaming someone or pardon them for what they have done and move on.

2 Reconciliation bringing people together who were opposed to each other.

Crime and punishment

89. The need for law and justice

1 The law is the rules made by Parliament which are enforced by the Police and courts.

2 A crime is an act against the law.

3 Agree:
- Yes the law is there for a reason.
- If we didn't have the law, we would have chaos.

Disagree:
- Sometimes it may be right to do something to help someone.
- The law can sometimes be wrong and need changing.

90. Theories of punishment

1 Deterrence is the idea that punishments should be of such a nature that they will put people off and deter them from committing crimes.

2 Agree:
- The criminal is punished, they are deterred from doing the same thing again and can reform.
- Justice is sought for the victim.

Disagree:
- Punishments aren't severe enough.
- Often many theories of punishment do not work and criminals reoffend.

91. Christians and justice

1 Agree:
- Everyone deserves to be treated the same and fairly.
- Jesus taught the Golden Rule – 'do to others what you would have them do to you' (Matthew 7:12).
- It is important to stand up against things which are wrong.

Disagree:
- There are more important things in life.
- Justice is never achieved so it is pointless.

2 Agree:
- Christians have a responsibility to stand up for people as this is what Jesus did.
- The Bible teaches that God wants people to behave justly.
- Jesus taught that everyone is equal and deserves respect (Golden Rule).

- On Judgement Day, God will judge Christians according to how they have behaved. If they have behaved justly they will be rewarded in Heaven.

Disagree:
- Everyone has a responsibility not just religious people.
- Religious people shouldn't have to if they do not agree with the action.
- They already do a lot to work towards justice.

92. Muslims and justice

1 Islam:
- The Qur'an teaches that God wants people to act justly towards each other.
- Everyone is equal under Islamic law.
- Justice is the basis of zakat (one of the five pillars), through tax on income, wealth is shared which makes society fairer and more just.
- Shari'ah law requires justice.
- Muhammad always acted justly.
- To please Allah. Muslims believe Allah is watching every action they perform so are conscious to help others and stand up against injustice.

93. Non-religious arguments about capital punishment

1
- The death penalty does not seem to stop other people committing the same crimes.
- Some people have been killed who were innocent.
- It is murder itself, whether you are religious or not, murder is always wrong and as bad as the criminal's original act.
- Human life is important and should never be taken.
- Terrorists who are executed can end up being seen as martyrs which can increase terrorist acts.
- Life imprisonment and other punishments are more effective.

94. Christian attitudes to capital punishment

1 Agree:
- The Old Testament teaches that capital punishment should be used for serious crimes.
- St Paul teaches (New Testament) that Christians should accept and obey the laws of the country they are in so this may include the death penalty.
- Jesus never taught that the death penalty was wrong.

Disagree:
- It goes against the sanctity of life.
- Jesus taught that revenge is wrong.
- The Ten Commandments teach that it is wrong to take a life and Christians should follow the teachings of the Bible.

2
- The Old Testament teaches that capital punishment should be used for serious crimes.
- Jesus never taught that the death penalty was wrong.
- St Paul taught that you should accept the laws of the country you live in so this may include the death penalty.
- The Church used the death penalty in the Middle Ages.

95. Muslim attitudes to capital punishment

1 Agree:
- The scholars of Shari'ah law cannot agree on the details of the death penalty.
- The Qur'an says that the death penalty is an option – it does not have to be used.
- Jesus taught Christians to 'Love thy neighbour'.

Disagree:
- The Qur'an states that the death penalty can be used for certain crimes.
- Shari'ah law agrees that it can be used for certain crimes.
- Muhammad seemed to agree with it.
- Muhammad sentenced people to death.

96. Drug and alcohol laws

1
- Drugs and alcohol can be damaging to a person's health (cancer, liver disease, mental illness).
- People can become addicted to drugs and alcohol which can lead to health problems and to social problems.
- Children need to be protected.
- Drugs can cause social problems.

97. Social and health problems caused by drugs and alcohol

1 Addiction is when a person is compelled to engage in something regardless of its bad effects.

2 Agree:
- It would protect children.
- It would help society and people's lives improve, by limiting access and therefore limiting addiction.

Disagree:
- It helps people to socialise and relax.
- People will always get it even if it is illegal.

98. Christian attitudes to drugs and alcohol

1 Do drink:
- The Bible does not forbid it.
- It is not illegal and Christians should follow the law of the country they live in.
- Jesus drank wine and turned water into wine at a wedding.
- Wine was used during the Last Supper.
- Many Churches do not forbid it (Holy Communion).

Don't drink:
- It can impair a person's judgement and their ability to act in a Christian way.
- There are many other types of drinks available today – you do not need to drink alcohol.
- The Bible teaches that God created human bodies and we should not abuse them so it is best to avoid health issues connected to drinking alcohol.

2 Agree:
- It can impair a person's judgement and their ability to act in a Christian way.
- There are many other types of drinks available today – you do not need to drink alcohol.
- Sanctity of life: God created human bodies and we should not abuse them so it is best to avoid health issues connected to drinking alcohol.

Disagree:
- The Bible does not forbid it.
- Jesus drank wine and turned water into wine at a wedding.
- Wine was used during the Last Supper.
- Many Churches do not forbid it.
- It is not illegal and Christians should follow the law of the country they live in.

99. Muslim attitudes to drugs and alcohol

1
- Sanctity of Life – humans were created by Allah so people should look after their bodies and not abuse them.
- The Qur'an teaches that intoxicants are forbidden.
- Muhammad taught about the dangers of alcohol and drugs and called them 'the mother of all sins'.
- The effects of drugs would mean Muslims would not be able to perform their religious duties correctly.

101. Unit 8 Exam skills: (a) questions

- The Golden Rule – the teaching of Jesus that you should treat others as you would like them to treat you.
- Pressure group – a group formed to influence government policy on a particular issue.
- Global warming – global warming is the increase in the temperature of the Earth's atmosphere.
- A sin is an act against the will of God.

102. Unit 8 Exam skills: (b) questions

1 Agree:
- Everyone lives on Earth so should take responsibility.
- If everyone helps, change can happen.
- Christians believe that humans have been given Stewardship of the Earth and we should after the creation of God.

Disagree:
- We should just enjoy the world and life.
- One person cannot make a difference.

103. Unit 8 Exam skills: (c) questions

1
- Christians believe they will be judged after death on their actions in their life so should behave in the way the Bible directs them as this is what God wanted.
- The Bible teaches that God is just and that people should behave in the same way.
- Jesus taught that everyone should be treated equally and fairly.
- Jesus taught the Golden Rule of treating others as you would want to be treated.
- Jesus taught that we should 'Love thy neighbour' meaning that we should care for each other, this would include treating everyone fairly.
- Christian churches teach that Christians should behave justly.

104. Unit 8 Exam skills: (d) questions

1 Agree:
- The Bible gives an overall message of peace ('If someone strikes you on the right cheek, turn to him the other also.' (Matthew 5:39), 'Love your enemies ...' (Matthew 5:44)).
- Christians believe they should work towards achieving peace.
- One of the titles given to Jesus was 'Prince of Peace' and Christians should follow his example.
- Jesus taught that people should love their enemies and innocent people should not suffer.
- Some Christians are pacifist because it is wrong to take a life of another (Ten Commandments).

Disagree:
- Sometimes violence may be necessary.
- Jesus told people they should obey the lawful government.
- Some Christians claim that it is right to have armed forces to protect the nation from enemies.
- The Qur'an teaches that war is right if you are attacked.
- Muhammad fought in wars and taught Muslims to fight in just wars.

Published by Pearson Education Limited, Edinburgh Gate, Harlow, Essex, CM20 2JE.

www.pearsonschoolsandfecolleges.co.uk

Copies of official specifications for all Edexcel qualifications may be found on the Edexcel website: www.edexcel.com

Edited by Samantha Jackman
Edited and produced by Wearset Ltd, Boldon, Tyne and Wear
Typeset by Jerry Udall and Wearset Ltd, Boldon, Tyne and Wear

Illustrated by KJA Artists
Cover illustration by Miriam Sturdee
Picture research by Caitlin Swain

First published 2012

16 15 14
10 9 8 7 6 5

British Library Cataloguing in Publication Data
A catalogue record for this book is available from the British Library

ISBN 978 1 446 90530 2

Printed in Slovakia by Neografia

Acknowledgements
The author and publisher would like to thank the following individuals and organisations for permission to reproduce photographs:

(Key: b-bottom; c-centre; l-left; r-right; t-top)

Alamy Images: Buddy Mays 45tl, itanistock 45bl; **Bridgeman Art Library Ltd:** Look and Learn 3t; **CAFOD:** 91r; **Christian Aid:** 91l; **Corbis:** ATEF HASSAN / Reuters 31b, Austrian Archives 80l, Chris Carroll 84; **Getty Images:** 43, 55, 59l, AFP 54l, 54r, 80r, 87, Brendan O'Sullivan 83t, Dario Mitidieri 3b, Gamma-Rapho via 95, Hill Street Studios / Blend Images 32b, ImagesBazaar 31t, Layland Masuda 25tr/2, Maria Ismawi 27, Megan Q Daniels 45tr, Michael Ochs Archives / Stringer 42b, UIG 93; **Islamic Relief:** 92; **Muslim Aid:** 92l; **Science Photo Library Ltd:** NEIL BROMHALL 63; **Shutterstock.com:** Andy Dean Photography 25bc, Anneka 18, Dima_Rogozhin 32t, Dubova 25bl, Monkey Business Images 25br/2, Omer N Raja 29, Piotr Marcinski 57r, wavebreakmedia ltd 25tl, Yuran 42t, Yuri Arcurs 70, Zurijeta 19; **United Nations:** 58

Every effort has been made to contact copyright holders of material reproduced in this book. Any omissions will be rectified in subsequent printings if notice is given to the publishers.

In the writing of this book, no Edexcel examiners authored sections relevant to examination papers for which they have responsibility.